THE TEN ORIGINAL SYSTEMS OF

YOGA

Ernest Wood

The Ten Original Systems of Yoga

Copyright © 2012 by Indo-European Publishing

All rights reserved.

Contact:
IndoEuropeanPublishing@gmail.com

The present edition is a reproduction of 1920 publication of this work, produced in the current edition with completely new, easy to read format by Indo-European Publishing.

ISBN: 978-1-60444-009-6

IndoEuropean
Publishing.com
Los Angeles, CA, USA

PREFACE

There are many people in America and Europe who want to know what yoga is, and they say, "Do not tell us about the yoga of one particular school; we want a concise survey of the whole field."

I have tried to address this need in the present small volume. In doing so I have endeavored to preserve the perfect authenticity and clearness of the original teachings of ten different well-known Oriental schools of yoga teaching and practice. This I am doing mainly direct from the original texts and with an extensive knowledge of their actual operation, acquired largely during my thirty-eight-years residence in the East.

Then comes the remark: "We want to find out whether there is anything in these forms of yoga which we can use in our present civilization. Has it anything for us?" It certainly has. In explanation of this reply, I will first mention that it will be seen by the reader of this book that reflectiveness and meditation play a large part in most of the yoga systems, and then add,

"Half an hour spent in meditation or even in reflection in the morning is not time wasted. It is not even time spent. It is time gained, because it will make the rest of the day far more fruitful than it would otherwise have been."

"How so?"

"It will do this in four ways:

"First, it will co-ordinate the contents of the mind on all aspects of the matters in which you are currently interested, and ensure that nothing is missed or overlooked.

"Secondly, it will permit the rising of new ideas, through the recombinations of old ones, and suggestions arising from them.

"Thirdly, it will exercise the mental faculty, and thus increase both its grip and its grasp, improving its functionality for the whole day, just as the muscular development acquired by ten minutes' exercise in the morning gives the body greater strength for the whole day.

"Fourthly, it will automatically work some of the magic of the mind, whereby you will be put tele-magnetically into touch with things and persons you are interested in, and thus it will create opportunities and even so-called coincidences."

If this is not enough, let us add that it will open new fields of interest, especially those which are concerned with the understanding and right use of life itself.

It will also enrich consciousness itself. Inasmuch as we all enjoy consciousness more than anything else it will be giving us the best of all benefits. There is a story about two men who were talking about a little boy who was licking an ice-cream cone. One remarked that the boy did not like ice-cream. The other, sensing a catch, said he supposed that what was meant by that remark was that what was liked was the taste of the ice-cream. But the reply was that what the boy really liked was only the consciousness of the taste of the ice-cream, and that applies to everything in our lives.

Why should not our subjective faculties be cultivated? We take care of our horses and other animals, and give them proper food, exercise and rest. Why not do the same for our mental faculties — also for our moral and spiritual ones, too, and that not merely by the way?

But to return to the material practicality of the subject. Thousands of people are breaking down in modern life because they cannot stand the pace. Suppose we can teach them how to keep up the pace of outward modern life but at the same time have such inner calm and poise that they can stand it without strain and fatigue. That is something well worth while, is it not? Well, this is not an idle promise. It is a fact.

But you must be warned. What you gain in yoga must be accompanied by goodwill towards others and the wish that they also may benefit in some way by your increased knowledge and power. Without this there will be a recoil on your head, just as sure as the magic of the magnetism of thought operates to benefit you. But that is no hardship, is it, when we all know full well in these enlightened days that there is no true pleasure in life when our neighbors or companions are suffering, and indeed almost the greatest of all pleasures is to see others happy. This nature of ours is not merely negative and concerned with sympathy for the suffering. It is also positive — the enjoyment of the happiness of others. Is that not why people like a peaceful country scene? As one lady remarked a few days ago: "How much nicer the meadow is now that the cows are in it!"

In the present world crisis most of us are concerned not so much with the idea that a bomb may fall on our own heads—we would rather it did so than on the heads of those near and dear to us, or on any considerable number of people anywhere. We are very much concerned about the plight of humanity in general. We rejoice over the prosperity of the average family of today, and we quake to think that it may be destroyed and an age of torment and slavery may engulf it. We think of the welfare of the children and the aged, and most of us would not enjoy a personal prosperity built upon the sufferings of these.

These are matters which yoga also puts before us, studies and explains, so that we learn that happiness is a matter not merely of physical, emotional and mental health and strength, and these in balance — no small matter — but of social and moral and ethical health and balance also, and even something more of which we know only the rudiments now, namely that which we call the spiritual self, from the consecration by which all the invigoration of our powers proceeds.

Let us be definite and certain about this. If by some personal suffering or loss you could stop for good and all the sort of war that took place in Korea — stop the maiming and killing of unbelligerent men, stop the ruin and slaughter of gentle people, the populations of admirable lands of ancient culture, such as Korea was — how far would you go in that loss and suffering? Most people would go to the limit. Does this not tell us that it is *ability* we lack, not *love* of our fellowmen? We are held back by helplessness, not by selfishness. If the issue could be squarely put, how many would shrink from the supreme sacrifice? Very few. It is the sort of thing Tom Paine asked the people of the American Colonies to do when George Washington was on the wrong side of victory, and most of them held off through that helpless feeling, but there were enough responses to turn the tide, and ensure the material establishment of a grand set of social ideals which are again in danger today.

Washington acted much because he had thought and felt much. We do not think enough—that is what is the matter. Let us have some practice and more know-how in thinking—that is what yoga can give to every one. Not to make the opposite error, to sink ourselves in thought, as some have done, but to invigorate and rationalize the whole of living by the awakening of more of man-ness in our minds.

The man-ness of man is constantly being surrendered to externals. This is one of the warnings of the yoga theoreticians. By a curious paradox of our life, the very service of mammon, as we may call it, is often the one thing which calls the man-ness of man into activity. I must explain. The human body has its more or less permanent set-up, with a group of pains and pleasures geared to its activities and designed primarily to warn it against dangers and tempt it into healthful activities, which have for the most part become automatic. When, for example, the needs of the body are satisfied with food, the natural appetite dies away for the time being, and if it is then stimulated artificially by exciting spices pain will arise after some time and tend to stop that excess. To correct this and numerous other troubles the man-ness of the man, in the shape of his power of thought and affection is aroused. But it is rather a pitiful situation that the man-ness of the man should be awakened and operated for such negative reasons, when it is really the activity of that man-ness which is the chief possibility of enjoyment in human life.

Thus we have heard recently a story of two boys who now, as men, are regarded as fine examples of the resolute betterment of human life. Briefly, they mortgaged everything they had and went into the silver fox business and made a lot of money. That was the betterment! And presumably they then settled down to a life of bodily enjoyment or bodily excitement, the chief feature of which could be described as the consciousness bathing, as it were, in the body's enjoyment. How different from the pursuit of knowledge, affection and art—which grow by exercise, and show us the man enjoying *himself*, or enjoying, to use my previous phrase, the man-ness of man, and thereby increasing his man-ness.

The paradox of the situation is resolved by the knowledge that all material gains *can be used* for the purposes of the real man that we all the time truly are, did we but observe and remember that important fact. It could be summed up in the old trinity of truth, goodness and beauty, resulting from the use of honest thought, affection and the will. And when they are so used there is more man-ness and in consequence more happiness.

Briefly, then, the great yogis do not teach abandonment of circumstances, but triumph over circumstances. The result is that man being true to himself overcomes all his troubles—of body, emotions and mind—and there is then harmony between the outer and the inner life. It could then be said that man does not serve mammon, but mammon serves him.

Now we must notice a very important principle of yoga, which arises from this recognition of the true nature of man. It is that in yoga practice there must be no negativity or passivity of the man. Anything in the nature of hypnotism, suggestion or auto-suggestion, repetition of words, sentences or ideas to form *habits* of thought or feeling is strictly taboo.

The emotions and the ideas which constantly spring up from past associations are to be used *under the surveillance of the real man* in all circumstances. With his present powers of thought, love and the will he will either permit them or change them, as the case may be, just as he permits or orders the body to walk or jump or talk on a given occasion, and does not expect it to follow old habits of activity but to keep quiet when he does not want it to do something. The body must be well treated, of course, like a good horse, but it is not supposed to run around the country-side on its own account. Similarly, the emotions and the mind should be quiet, having only that functional flow which in them is analogous to the movements of breathing, heart action, digestion etc. in the body.

This matter of *no passivity* appears very clearly in the practice of concentration, meditation and contemplation. Concentration is *voluntary attentiveness* to something. This brings about a contraction which is at the same time an intensification of consciousness, somewhat analogous to placing a reflector round a lamp. Meditation, which proceeds as soon as concentration is established, is an *expansion of attention* to the object *without loss of this intensification*. It thus consists of a flow or fountain of observation and thought about the object. When this process is complete it can be followed by an *active poise* of the mind, without any passivity, which is contemplation. At the end of the meditation it will be observed, the thinking stops. Then the *new process* — a third process — must go on without any diminution of the high quality or intensity of consciousness obtained by the concentration or voluntary attention. If the reader tries this method with some perseverance he will soon find the benefit of it, in the consciousness, in the powers of the mind (will, love and thought) and in the body and his world of things and events.

It will soon be found that this three-fold meditation, practiced at first at special times, begins to work with great swiftness even in the midst of activity, and even amid what were previously regarded as disturbing circumstances. In this connection one wishes again to issue the warning that increase of knowledge and power without love will lead to a point of great recoil. No organism can continue if it develops one or two of its functions at the expense of the rest—that is obvious in the body, which to be healthy must have harmoniousness and balance in all its parts. This is true with regard to the three parts of the man-ness of us. One cannot know everything, love everything, do everything, but what one does in the small area of a human being's life must be *positive* in thought, love and the will. There can be no hate and such emotions, no carelessness of judgment, no surrender of the will, all of which imply negativity and waste of man-ness. There can and indeed must be relaxation, but this also must be voluntary. Voluntary relaxation carried on with your approval, sometimes with your assistance. Another question is, "What is the relation between mysticism and yoga?"

In connection with this we have to think of yoga as goal—not only as methods or the way to the goal. The goal of yoga is the Beyond. Some call this God. God is the Beyond. This word Beyond only is used in the *Bhagavad Gita* for what in the West we call the goal or God. To know the Beyond and to enter the Beyond are familiar expressions. If someone asks what God is we cannot in these enlightened days say "He is a big man, an exacting but benevolent old gentleman with a white beard," nor even, "He is a great mind, a great thinker and lover and law-giver." We have to admit that God is the *Beyond*, beyond both world and mind, *beyond object and subject*, and therefore a Mystery, except to those who have experience of the Beyond. The very word mystic means "with the eyes closed"—in terms of yoga we say with the eyes of the body and the eyes of the mind—both sets—closed. There are, of course, mystic eyes belonging to the Beyond. That is another truth. Man has them, but scarcely knows it, and so has in most cases still to learn to use them. He is sometimes reminded that he has them by the rare God-knowers of past or present.

One last question: "Why Oriental yoga? Why not merely yoga? Surely this yoga cannot be Oriental or Occidental, any more than science or, strictly, religion, or the good life."

The answer is that many Eastern thinkers and writers have dealt with this subject, and have left us books explaining it. That is all we mean by the word Oriental in this matter. Those books have their individual emphasis on the use and study of thought or of love—the human feeling—or the will, but all concur in the nature of the goal. The subject has not been dealt with so extensively in the new civilizations of Europe and America, which have been mostly engaged in building a satisfactory material life. Let us therefore blend the knowledge from the Orient with the culture of body and environment which we have derived from Greece and the culture of the heart which has been accepted from Palestine.

ERNEST WOOD

Bethel,
Connecticut
November, 1953

TABLE OF CONTENTS

INTRODUCTION

THE TEN ORIENTAL YOGAS

There is great interest in the Western world at the present time on the subject of Oriental Occultism, and very rightly so, for the time has come for it to be blended in with the practical material civilization which has been so wonderfully developed in the modern world. There will be two benefits in this blending—more success in the outer world and more peace in the inner life. The time has gone for any of us—East or West—to think of Occultism as an escape from material reality and responsibility into some vague inner condition in which one retreats from all that material life stands for. Rather it is concerned in the purpose voiced by Emerson when he wrote: "To make in matter home for mind." To make of this world a place where consciousness can enjoy to the full all the powers of its own mind and at the same time discover that there is more to the mind than is commonly known—that is practical Occultism.

To know how the mind works we cannot do better than turn to the ancient writers on what is called yoga—looking at *all* the principal ancient schools of yoga, not only one or two of them. Of these there are seven well-known surviving schools in India today, and in addition to these our survey of Oriental Occultism would be incomplete without allusion to three others—the Persian Sufis, the Buddhist "Noble Way," and the Chinese and Japanese Zen. This makes ten in all.

Many are the modern teachers of practical occultism or yoga, but all of them can be classed as especially devoted to the methods of one or other of these modes of practice.

Why have we at the outset associated the word yoga with occultism? Because yoga is the practice of occult powers—or rather the discovery and use of those powers residing unseen in the depths of the human mind. The practice could begin with the formula, "We are only part alive," and from that standpoint proceed to investigate the Introspectional Psychology of the ancients, which they said united them—yoga means union—with the latent possibilities and unseen actualities of and beyond the mind. The Introspectional Psychology, all the ancient teachers asserted, is justified by its results; it works.

That it should have been developed in elder times, in very peaceful times, in the Orient, was very natural. In those very settled days there were whole classes of society who had leisure to give to these matters. There were not only solitary and silent hermit-investigators, but also teachers with small schools, and traveling lecturers, and occasional conferences of teachers organized by the ancient rulers. But nowadays we have a phase of material activity, most fully developed in America and now invading the Orient itself, which leaves people with little energy or time to carry on the studies in Introspectional Psychology in which many people formerly immersed themselves—in which they were often at fault when they made the delights of the mind a substitute for the valuable experience of the whole estate of man. This modern activity is such that very often people have nervous breakdowns of various kinds. Many must be the material achievements left unfulfilled because of the collapse of those who could originate them but could not bear the strain of carrying them to their completion.

It is into this field of sorrow, lit up only occasionally by success, that the Oriental occultism can be brought for the discovery and use of the inner resources of the mind, increasing the power and improving the machinery of thought, emotion and the will. That peace and power are two aspects of one principle is one of the chief discoveries of the Oriental occultist—a discovery within the reach of all reasonable persons.

It is not to be thought, however, that the ancient teachers alluded to are proposing some sort of magic as a substitute for our present method of doing things through the mechanism of a healthy body. That the magic exists is true, and there is a long list of "psychic powers" which manifest themselves in various degrees quite naturally as the process of yoga goes on, but the teachers mostly refer to these as not of great value, and advise against making the mind a "playground" for them. In India there are many who can exhibit varieties of hallucinatory or hypnotic effects, and also telepathy, psychometry, clairvoyance, clairaudience, levitation, astral traveling, transportation and apport, and similar occult or magical arts. Indeed, some people with very little education in other respects have been specially trained in one or more of these faculties and powers, so that they are able to astonish the tourist and earn a living by exhibiting these feats. But the real yogis are not interested in these. They are interested in mastering environment and finding the ethical and spiritual forces and experiences which are not only immature but positively infantile in most people.

It will be asked: "Why do not these more perfect men use both the higher powers and the magics?" The answer is, "They do. They use these constantly, but they do not display them, for they know that very many persons would be tempted out of the regular course of their evolution by the glamour of these faculties and powers. And many would use them as only another additional means for exploiting their fellow men." As to such matters as applying a healing influence for body and mind — these can be as well used in silence as with any display. I remember that one very respected Hindu occultist, when questioned on this point said that if highly successful and convincing demonstrations of the occult powers were given, most people would be overcome by modesty and would want to lean upon the demonstrator, others would be frightened, others would call it the work of the devil, and some who had not seen for themselves would call it all a fraud—but on the other hand those who sincerely practice the yoga will invariably have before long some convincing experiences of their own, useful for their own private encouragement and essential benefit.

In my book *The Occult Training of the Hindus*, published some years ago in Madras, and recently reprinted there, I presented a brief survey of this subject, resulting from my long residence in India, during which I was chiefly interested in studying these matters. In that book I have told of my acquaintance and friendship with many of these exponents of yoga, and how I thus learned that all over the country there are tens of thousands of people who give part of their day to the pursuit of the methods of the ancient occult teachers, although they are engaged in modern occupations. There is in India, I would say, a vein of practicality in these matters which most Western persons just do not understand.

In the present small volume, intended to bring these matters more to the attention of the West, I am making use again of much of the material in that book, without feeling it necessary to employ quotation marks. This has been done considerably in Chapters 2 to 6. Chapters 7 to 9 are entirely newly written.

Let us begin then with the statement that the seven well-known varieties of yoga practice among the Hindus can be listed as follows: —

1. The Raja Yoga of Patanjali.

2. The Karma and Buddhi Yoga of Shri Krishna.

3. The Gnyana Yoga of Shri Shankaracharya.

4. Hatha Yoga.

5. Laya Yoga.

6. Bhakti Yoga.

7. Mantra Yoga.

These seven can be classified in two groups—the first three being called varieties of *raja-yoga* and the last four varieties of *hatha-yoga*. The adjective *raja* means "kingly" because the man becomes king or master of his own faculties. The last four emphasize the importance of material aids, by working largely on the outside or on the "terrestrial man," which is composed of the body along with its bundle of habitual emotions and memories and knowledge.

The *raja-yogi* maintains that the inner powers of the mind can never be enhanced by any external means, but only by their own exercise.

Here the law of growth from within is paramount. By the use of thought, thought grows. This is true also of love and the will. There is no other way in which these growths can be obtained. A realization of this fact sets the novice on his own feet, and cures him at the outset of any tendency to lean or depend upon others, even upon experts and teachers he may admire.

Still, this exercise can be hindered or at least made very difficult by any bad condition of the body in such matters as nervous disorders, irregular breathing, bad balance, and undue tension. The *hatha-yogis* of the more intellectual kind accede to the proposition that all higher growth is from within, but still say "No *raja* without *hatha*" because they find that bodies generally require some preparation.

The thorough-going *raja-yogis* however, generally reply that there is *raja* without *hatha*, and in fact that *raja-yoga* if properly done will itself put the body in order, for the mind influences the body even if the body cannot influence the mind. Still there is no harm, they often add, in just a little *hatha-yoga* as well, provided that the aspirant does not fall into a state of dependence on anything or any person, and does not seek merely the comforts of the body, emotions and knowledge, or make his purpose the increase of his power with a view to gain in these three fields.

The term *hatha-yoga*, when used strictly, refers specifically only to the fourth school on our list, for it is specially devoted to breathing practices, dealing with the incoming and outgoing—or *ha* and *tha* breaths. But the term is quite elastic and portions of the remaining three groups of teachings are generally included, to supplement the breathing exercises of the *hatha-yoga* schools. Inasmuch as all the four schools operate by external means they are all classable as in the general field of *hatha-yoga*, as they all work on the body and environment.

One of the great gains of modern yoga is that the "hair shirt" has been entirely given up. The new race is not afraid of the world. It does not regard it as evil or of the devil. Modern man can trust himself amidst all the lures. He can handle them and be their master. He knows his own powers and can very well judge the results of his use of them. He can envisage a metaphysical goal and also be aware of the metaphysical in the physical as he goes along. He feels that whatever he may gain by any exercise or experience in his will, his goodwill and his intelligence is all to the good, quite apart from any so-called material gain, and there is no objection to that in addition. If he is caught up in any interests, enthusiasms or excitements—as he is—he knows not to go too far, and that he will come out of them richer in character, even if a bit scarred. He knows that time will heal all the wounds and ripen the character. So in the field of yoga today he is not in fear of missing anything, nor dependent upon a particular guide, but will choose his exercises with all the natural confidence with which he can choose a good cigar. He asks for information, not gifts, nor orders, and here the Orient spreads it out before him for his choice. According to individual temperament each will choose, and then travel in the way that suits him best.

CHAPTER 1

PATANJALI'S RAJA YOGA

Foremost among the Yoga teachings of India comes that of Patanjali dating back, according to popular tradition, to at least 300 B.C. His *Yoga Sutras* give definitions and instructions which are accepted by all teachers, even when they also make additions in minor matters. He begins with a description of yoga as "*Chitta vritti nirodha.*" *Chitta* is the mind, the instrument that stands between the man and the world. As a gardener uses a spade for digging, so a man uses the mind for dealing with the world. Acted upon by the things of the outer world through the senses, it presents to the man within a picture of those things, as on the plate of a camera. Acted upon by the will of the man within, it transmits into action in the body the thought-power that is its positive characteristic. It thus has two functions—one receptive or negative, the other active or positive. It transmits from the world to the man within, and also from the man within to the outer world.

Vritti means literally a whirlpool, and *nirodha* signifies restraint or control. Thus yoga practice is control of the whirlpools or changes of the mind or, in simple terms, voluntary direction of what is commonly called thought, or control of the ideas which are in the mind.

The mind of the average man is far from being an instrument within his control. It is being impressed at all times, even during sleep to some extent, with the pictures of a thousand objects clamoring for his attention, through ears, skin, eyes, nose and mouth, and by telepathic impressions from others. In addition to all that, it is in a state of agitation on its own account, bubbling in a hundred places with disturbing visions, excited by uncontrolled emotion or worrying thoughts. Let him achieve control of all this, says Patanjali, and his reward will be that he shall stand in his own state.

That a man should be in his own true state has two meanings: first, that in his repose he will be utterly himself, not troubled with the whirlpools, which, however slight, are in the eyes of the yogi nothing but worry, and secondly, that in his activity as a man, using the mind, he will be a positive thinker, not merely a receptacle for impressions from outside and ideas which he has collected in the course of time.

Ideas in the mind should be material for thought, not merely ideas, just as the muscles are useful means of action, not mere lumps of flesh. To be a positive thinker, lover and willer, master in one's own house, is to be oneself, in one's own true state; all the rest is slavery or bondage, willing or unwilling. To its master, the man, the *vrittis* of *chitta* are always only objects of knowledge, because of his not being involved in them, say Aphorisms iv 18-20. These *vrittis* are ideas or items in the mind.

The final aim of Patanjali's yoga is to cease this slavery and achieve freedom. The technical name for this great achievement is *kaivalya*, independence. That is really only another name for divinity, for material things are in bondage, unable to move of themselves, and always moved by forces from the outside; but the divine is by definition free, able to move of itself. Every man feels in himself some spark of that divine freedom, which he then calls the will, and that is the power with which he can control his mind.

In Patanjali's yoga the aspirant uses his will in self-control. Thought governs things, we know; so much so that every voluntary movement of the body follows a mental picture; therefore all work done by us, even with the hands, is done by thought-power. But will controls thought, concentrates it, expands it, causes its flow—directs, in fact, its three operations of concentration, meditation, and contemplation. The perfection of these three is the aim of the Patanjali yoga exercises.

Before proceeding with the systematic description of the practices of yoga, which begins in his Book ii, Patanjali mentions two things which are necessary for success in controlling the *vrittis* or thoughts, namely *abhyasa* and *vairagya*. *Abhyasa* means constant practice in the effort to secure steadiness of mind. *Vairagya* is that condition of the feelings in which they are not colored by outside things, but are directed only by our own best judgment. This detachment of the emotions may be "lower" or "higher" according as it is born from dislike of external conditions, or from a vision of the glorious joy of the pure free life. The higher uncoloredness leads to the highest contemplation, and therefore to freedom, the goal of this yoga. Patanjali's systematic instruction for practical training is given in two portions. The first part, called *Kriya Yoga*, is often translated as preliminary yoga because a person who has not first practiced it is not likely to succeed in the main portion, the *ashtanga*, or "eight limbs" of yoga practice. But it is much more than preliminary. It is the yoga of action, the yoga which must be practiced all the time in daily life. Without it, meditation would be useless, for yoga involves not retirement or retreat but a change in attitude towards the world. It. is in the midst of life's activities that our freedom must be realized, for to desire to slip away into some untroubled sphere would be mere escape, a perpetuation of the dream of the best we have so far learned to know, a denial of the possibility of our real freedom. A man must become master of himself, whatever other people and beings, whose activities constitute the major portion of his world, may do.

The object of the preliminary yoga or yoga of action is to weaken what are called the five *kleshas*. A *klesha* is literally an affliction, just as one would speak of a crooked spine or blindness as an affliction. The five afflictions are *avidya*, *asmita*, *raga*, *dwesha* and *abhinivesha*, which may be translated ignorance, egotism, liking and disliking, and possessiveness. One leading ancient commentator on the Aphorisms, named Vyasa, states that these, when active, bring one under the authority of Nature, and produce instability, a stream of causes and effects in the world, and dependence upon others. They are faults of the man himself, not outside causes of trouble; the world can never hurt us, except through our own faults, and these five reduce us to pitiful slavery. Having submitted to these, a man is constantly moved from outside, governed too much by circumstances. "Ignorance" describes all those activities of the mind which do not take into account the fact that man is in himself eternal, pure and painless. The man who does not accept his own true nature as eternal, pure and painless, will judge and value all objects improperly. A house, a chair and a pen are something to a man, by which he can satisfy his body and mind. They could not be the same things to a cow. But the question now is: what are all these things to the real man, who is eternal, pure and painless? To look at all things as for the use of such a being is to begin to see them without error. It is to have true motives.

"Egotism" is the tendency to think "I am this," and the desire that other people also should think one to be this or that. Thinking oneself to be a certain object or mind, or the combination of these even in the form of an excellent and useful personality, means attachment to things. We are not a personality, but we possess one, and it is not to be despised if it is useful to the real man.

The error of Self-personality or egotism leads to the next two afflictions which are personal liking and disliking. These two are those unreasoning impulses which lead men to judge and value things by their influence on the comforts and pleasures and prides of the personality, not according to their value for an immortal being.

The fifth affliction is "possessiveness," beginning with clinging to the body, which indicates the lack of that insight which causes a man to regard the body as a mere instrument which he is willing to use, and wear out in the course of time.

In this affliction we have not merely the fear of death, but that of old age as well, for men forget that the bodily life has its phases—childhood, youth, manhood and old age—and each of these has its own perfections, though it has not the perfections of the other stages. In this course there is constant apparent loss as well as gain, because no man can pay full attention to all the lessons of life at once, or exert at the same time all his faculties, any more than a child in school can properly think of geography, history and mathematics in the period which is devoted to music.

In Hindu life, before it was disturbed from the West, men were wise enough in old age to give the family business into the hands of their mature sons, and devote themselves to the study and contemplation of life; and just as in the West it is considered the bounden duty of parents to support their children with every kindness and give them the opportunities that their stage in life requires, so it was always considered in the East the duty of the grown up children to support their old people with every kindness, treat them with honor and dignity as the source of their own opportunity and power, and give them every opportunity that *their* stage of life requires. The material requirements of these retired people were very small—a corner in the home, some food and occasional clothes.

It is not presumed that in the preliminary stages the candidate will completely destroy the five afflictions. His object will be attained if he succeeds in definitely weakening them. Three kinds of practices are prescribed for this purpose in the yoga of action. These are called *tapas, swadhyaya* and *ishwara-pranidhana*. It is impossible to translate these terms by a single word each, without causing serious misunderstanding. The first is often translated as austerity, and sometimes even as mortification. The word means literally "heat" and the nearest English equivalent to that when it is applied to human conduct is "effort." The yogi must definitely do those things that are good, even when a special effort is necessary because old habits of the personality stand in the way. Briefly it means this: "Do for the body what you know to be good for it. Do not let laziness, selfishness, or thoughtlessness stand in the way of your doing what you can to make the body and mind healthy and efficient."

Patanjali does not explain the practice of *tapas,* but Shri Krishna says, in the seventeenth chapter of the *Bhagavad Gita* "Reverential action towards the gods, the educated, the teachers and the wise, purity, straightforwardness, continence, and harmlessness are *tapas* of the body; speech not causing excitement, truthful, affectionate and beneficial, and used in self-study is the *tapas* of speech; clearness of thinking, coolness, quietness, self-control, and purity of subject-matter are the *tapas* of mind."

Shri Krishna here gives a wider range to the meaning of *tapas* than does Patanjali, who makes it particularly a matter concerning the body.

How than can any one say that *tapas* is self-torture? It is true that there has grown up a system of painful practices, such as that of holding the arm still until it withers, or sitting in the sun in the midst of a ring of fires, but these are superstitions which have grown up round a valuable thing, as they are liable to do everywhere. Those who follow these methods are few as compared with the true yogi. All over the country there are Indian gentlemen—many of them Government servants who have a routine task with short working hours—who every day spend some time in meditation, deliberately guiding themselves by the "Yoga Sutras."

A great example of *tapas* is that of the modern women. Their will-power in the government of their bodies and in overcoming bodily self-indulgence excites the greatest admiration. And their results are entirely in line with Patanjali's aphorism iii 45 in which he approves of "excellence of body" and refers to it as consisting of correct form, charm, strength and very firm well-knitness, all of which is the very reverse of mortification or self-castigation, which some have erroneously attributed to yoga, because of superstition.

These delightful beings are not even willing to leave Nature just as she is, but consider in many ways how to bring lightness and freedom from earthiness or grossness or clumsiness into bodily living and bodily appearance. Even the artificialities of high heels and very slender figures have the same "spiritual" background, and where excess or unbalance occurs it can at least be credited to good intentions, carried out with great will-power or *tapas*. The proportion of *tapas* is on the increase all the time as seen by the exercises and dietary courses which are extensively advertised and the thoroughness and continuity with which they are carried out.

Man himself, too, it must be said, shares a little in this sort of effort, shaving or at least trimming his beard and whiskers, and padding his shoulders to ridiculous excess, as he used to do his calves in the old days when trousers were worn short and stockings were the vogue.

In all these matters there has been plenty of *effort*, in the main tending away from uncouth and un-mastered living. I know some of both sexes who assiduously perform what our yogis call *uddiyana*, the exercises of the abdominal muscles, with the effect of correct posture and adequate strength, thus attaining the "natural corset," as it has been called, essential to health and good appearance. There is no doubt that such exercises are necessary for those who do not do work involving bending, and it is not a bad thing that this undertaking calls for considerable will-power which then becomes useful also for other purposes as well, and also contributes to the enjoyment of consciousness.

The second practice, *swadhyaya*, means the study of books that really concern yourself as an immortal being. Psychology, philosophy and ethics come in here. Give up indiscriminate reading, and study what bears upon your progress, is the advice.

The third practice, *ishwara-pranidhana*, means devotion to God, but God as understood by the Hindu, as the perfect Being pervading all things, the life of the world, the inner impulse of which each one of us is a *share*. The aspirant must habituate himself to see that Principle in everything, to accept all as from that hand. "Everything that is received is a gift," says a Hindu proverb; more than that, it is a gift from God, presented with perfect wisdom, to be accepted, therefore, with cheerfulness and joy. Behind the eyes of every person he meets, the aspirant must also see the Divine. The common salutation of the Hindu, with the palms together, looks curious to the Westerner, as resembling prayer. It *is* prayer—the recognition of God within our fellow-man. It is appreciation, the opposite of depreciation. *Ishwara-pranidhana* is in effect the full appreciation of everything. It makes for maximum attentiveness and thus maximum living.

This practice develops right feeling towards everything; the previous one right thought, and the first right use of the will, and the three together, pursued diligently for even a short time, play havoc with the five afflictions.

When the candidate has weakened the afflictions to some extent, he is ready for Patanjali's regular course, the eight "limbs" of yoga. These may be divided into three sets: two moral, three external, and three internal, as shown in the following list:—

1.	*Yama,*	Five abstentions.	Ethical
2.	*Niyama.*	Five observances.	
3.	*Asana.*	Balanced posture.	External
4.	*Pranayama.*	Regularity of breath.	
5.	*Pratyahara.*	Withdrawal of senses.	
6.	*Dharana.*	Concentration.	Internal
7.	*Dhyana.*	Meditation.	
8.	*Samadhi.*	Contemplation.	

The two ethical or moral "limbs" of yoga contain five rules each, which the man must practice in his daily life. Put together, they make what we may call "the ten commandments." The first five are; "Thou shalt not (a) injure, (b) lie, (c) steal, (d) be sensual and (e) be greedy."

Explaining this aphorism, Vyasa says that *ahimsa* or non-injury is placed first because it is the source of the following nine. Thus the brotherhood principle is considered as fundamental. Truth, for example, can hardly arise unless there is a motive beyond selfish desires. Vyasa explains that this means word and thought being in accordance with facts to the best of our knowledge. Only if speech is not deceptive, confused or empty of knowledge, he says, is it truth, because speech is uttered for the purpose of transferring one's knowledge to another.

Vachaspati's glossary interprets truth as word and thought in accordance with facts, and fact as what is really believed or understood by us on account of our own direct experience, our best judgment or the accepted testimony of reliable witnesses. So yoga is rooted in virtue, and that in brotherhood, or a feeling for others. Without at least the desire for these five, though perfection in them may not be attained, contemplation cannot yield its richest fruits. We are to be at peace with the world, even if the world is not at peace with us. In this case there is no *desire* to injure, lie, steal etc. Such activities are not sources of pleasure, in any circumstances.

The second five are: "Thou shalt be (a) clean, (b) content, (c) self-controlled, (d) studious, and (e) devoted." Few comments are needed on these. Contentment does not mean satisfaction, but willingness to accept things as they are and to make the most of them. Without dissatisfaction one would not take to yoga. It implies a desire to improve one's life. The remaining three are *tapas, swadhyaya* and *ishwara-pranidhana*, the preliminary yoga or yoga of daily life—apart from any private exercises—still carried on.

By the attainment of these five a man can be at peace with the world. It is the end of antagonism *from his side*.

Incidentally, Patanjali mentions that when the ten virtues are firmly established in a person's character definite effects will begin to appear, such as absence of danger, effectiveness of speech, the arrival of unsought wealth, vigor of body and mind, understanding of life's events, clarity of thought, steadiness of attention, control of the senses, great happiness, perfection of body and senses, intuition and realization of one's true self. These can come only after the cessation of all antagonisms to anybody or anything in the world.

Now we come to what some will regard as the more practical steps, though to the understanding yogi nothing can be more practical than the ten commandments. Of these the three external steps are *asana, pranayama* and *pratyahara*. The first is right posture, the second right breathing and the third control of the senses. They mean the training of the outer instrument or body so that it will offer no impediment to the serious practices of meditation which are to be taken up.

First, one must learn to sit quite still in a chosen healthy position. "The posture must be steady and pleasant," says Patanjali—that is all. There is no recommendation of any particular posture, least of all any distorted, painful, or unhealthy position. Posture is achieved when it becomes effortless and the mind easily forgets the body. It is chiefly a matter of balance. Some practice of balanced sitting, whether on the ground or on a chair is necessary until balanced musculature is attained. Very often there is fatigue because some of the muscles are weak, yet to sit unbalanced for long is almost impossible.

Next, regulation of breath is necessary. During meditation, people often forget to breathe normally; sometimes they breathe out and forget to breathe in again, and so are suddenly recalled to earth by a choking at the throat. Many people never breathe well and regularly at all; let them practice simple natural exercises, such as those recommended by teachers of singing, and take care that the body is breathing regularly and quietly before they enter their meditation. Sometimes numbers or proportionate times are prescribed, and one of the most authoritative in India is that in which one breathes in with the number 1, holds the breath with the number 4, breathes out with the number 2, and immediately begins again; but it is impossible to prescribe the perfect numbers, because they must differ with different people. The question really is: how long must your breath be so as to provide for enough oxidation? Science will some day say. But one must not hold it in longer than that, for to do so is to deprive the whole system of oxygen. Your body has to carry on all its ordinary sub-conscious activities while meditation is going on.

The only general practical advice one can give is that the breathing should be regular and a little slow, and there should be enough pause between in-breathing and out-breathing. It should also be calm, as may be judged by its not causing much disturbance in the outside air. The student will soon find out what suits him. Stunts such as breathing up one nostril and down the other, or holding the breath for a long time, are not mentioned by Patanjali and should be generally avoided as dangerous.

Pratyahara is the holding back of the senses from the objects of sense. One must practice paying no attention to sounds or sights or skin sensations, quietening the senses so that they will create no disturbance during meditation.

Think of what happens when you are reading an interesting book. Someone may come into the room where you are, may walk past you to get something, and go out again; but perhaps you heard and saw nothing at all. You were in what is sometimes called a brown study. The ears were open and the waves of sound in the air were no doubt agitating the tympanum, from which the nerves were carrying their message to the brain. The eyes were open, and the light waves were painting their pictures on the retina—but you saw and heard nothing, because your attention was turned away from those sensations.

The yogi must try to withdraw attention at will, so that in his meditation no sight or sound will distract him. This is helped by an absence of curiosity about anything external during the time set apart for meditation. One way of practicing this is to sit and listen for a while to the various sounds of nature; then listen to the delicate sound in the ear and so forget the former (though you cannot watch yourself forgetting it); then listen to a mere mental sound conjured up by the imagination, and so forget even the music in the ear.

Then come the three internal steps, to which everything else has been leading up, called *dhurana*, *dhyana* and *samadhi*. They are concentration, meditation, and contemplation.

Concentration is really voluntary attentiveness, but this involves narrowing the field of view, focusing the mental eye upon a chosen object. When you practice concentration or meditation, always choose the object before you begin. Sometimes people sit down and then try to decide what to concentrate upon, and come to no settled decision before their time is all gone. Then, do not try to *hold* the object in position by your thought. It is not the object that is going to run away; it is the mind that wanders. Let the object be thought of as in a natural position—if it is a pen it may be lying on the table; if it is a picture it may be hanging on the wall. Then narrow the field of attention down to it, and look at it with perfect calmness, and without any tension or sensation in the body or head.

Do not be surprised or annoyed if other thoughts intrude on your concentration. Be satisfied if you do not lose sight of your chosen object, if it remains the central thing before your attention. Take no notice of the intruding thoughts. Say "I do not care whether they are there or not." Keep the emotions calm in this manner, and the intruders will disappear when you are not looking. Calmness—no physical strain— is necessary for successful concentration, and, given this, it is not at all the difficult thing that it is sometimes supposed to be. Detailed methods for practicing concentration are given in my book *Concentration*," and regarding that and the other seven steps as well in my *Practical Yoga: Ancient and Modern*, which contains my translation and explanation of all the Patanjali Yoga aphorisms.

Meditation is a continuous flow or fountain of thought with regard to the object of your concentration. It involves the realization of that object as fully as possible. You must not let the string of thought go so far away on any line that the central object is in any way dimmed. On the contrary, every new idea that you bring forward must be fully thought of only with reference to it and should make it clearer and stronger than before. Thus for practice you might meditate on a cat. You would consider it in every detail; think of all its parts and qualities, physical, emotional, mental, moral and spiritual; think of its relation to other animals and of particular cats that you have known. When this is done you should know what a cat is much better than you did before. You will have brought into agreement and union all your knowledge or information on the subject. In this meditation there is no clutching, no anxiety, only calm mental reviewing and thinking.

The same method applies to virtues such as truth, kindness and courage. Many people have the most imperfect ideas as to what these are. Make concrete pictures in the imagination of acts of kindness, courage, truth. Then try to realize the states of emotion and mind, and the moral condition involved, and in doing so keep up the vividness of consciousness that has already been attained in the beginning of the practice on account of concentration on the concrete scene.

In meditation you take something up, but it is the opposite of going to sleep, because you *retain* the vivid qualities of reality which belong to the concentrated waking state. Yet it should always be done with perfect calm, and no tension or excitement. It widens, includes and integrates without loss of the quality gained by concentration or specific attentiveness.

Contemplation is another kind of concentration; this time a poise of the mind at the top end of your line of thought. When in meditation you have reached the highest and fullest thought you can about the chosen object, and your mind begins to waver, do not try to go forward, but do not fall back. Hold what you have attained, and poise calmly on it for a little time.

You will find that by contemplation you have created a platform. You have been making a new effort and so have developed or discovered some hitherto latent possibilities. There may be something in the nature of illumination. You must see what comes; never try to predetermine it. Then contemplation opens the door of the mind to intuitive knowledge, and many powers.

The student is told always to begin with concentration, then proceed to meditation. The triple process is a mind-poise called *sanyama*.

If the candidate wants to have what are commonly called psychic faculties and powers, Patanjali explains how he may obtain them by *sanyama* on various objects having corresponding qualities. He mentions knowledge of past and future, memory of past lives, reading of others' minds, perception of those who have reached perfection, and other powers and knowledge connected with "higher hearing, touch, sight, taste and smell" but remarks that, though these are accomplishments of the out-going mind, they are obstacles to the full or higher *samadhi*. Vachaspati comments on this that sometimes the mind is captivated by these psychic powers, just as a beggar may think of the possession of a little wealth as abundant riches, but the real yogi will reject them all. How can the real man, he asks, who has determined to remove all pain—including psychological or emotional pains—take pleasure in such accomplishments, which are opposed to his true state of being? Only by non attachment to all such things, however great, may the seeds of bondage be destroyed, and independence or freedom be attained.

True contemplation, poised on higher matters, Patanjali teaches, leads to the complete dispersal of the afflictions, and on to great clarity and insight, culminating in the cessation of the junction of the seer and the sight, the absence of all pain and the uncovering of the inner light.

CHAPTER 2

SHRI KRISHNA'S GITA-YOGA

We have used the new term Gita-Yoga here because it sums up the titles of all the eighteen chapters of the *Bhagavad Gita*, each of which is called a yoga, such as "The Yoga of Knowledge," "The Yoga of Action," etc.

Gita means song, and the whole title means the song of Shri Krishna, who is referred to as the Bhagavan—the most illustrious being. Shri Krishna is regarded as the most perfect of all Teachers—so much so that he could speak about everything from the divine standpoint and with divine knowledge of the reality beyond mind, so that when saying "I" he spoke as an incarnation of the Divine Being. He is considered to have lived about 5050 years ago, and the *Bhagavad Gita* is regarded as a record of what he said or sang to his devoted friend and disciple Arjuna, who was in a state of despondency because he could not solve a problem of "right or wrong" in which his emotions were very much involved. The problem was whether to fight or not in a certain battle which was about to begin. Arjuna's particular problem does not concern us now. The yoga-teaching it called forth from Shri Krishna is read and meditated upon by millions of people every day.

Shri Krishna's teaching is more a yoga for the emotions than the mind, although he does explain the necessity for mind-control and uses the same two words—practice (*abhyasa*) and uncoloredness (*vairagya*) for describing the means to its attainment as Patanjali does when starting his teaching. Shri Krishna tells Arjuna that though his heart is in the right place his unhappy emotional state is due to ignorance. The first point of the Teacher's instruction is—do not judge right and wrong from the standpoint of bodily appearances, but only from what is of value to the immortal soul, taking into account that actions, emotions, thoughts and decisions all have some effect, some tending downwards or away from self-realization and others tending upwards or toward self-realization. Downwards there is bondage and sorrow; upwards there is joy and freedom or the divine state of being, so let this first point be firmly understood at the beginning. Shri Krishna said: "You have sorrowed for those who need no sorrow, yet you speak words of wisdom. Those who know do not grieve for the living, nor for the dead. Certainly never at any time was I not, nor you, nor these lords of men, nor shall we ever cease to be hereafter. As there is for the owner of the body childhood, youth and old age in this body, so there comes another body; the intelligent man is not confused by that. Just as a man, having cast off his worn-out clothes, obtains others which are new, so the owner of the body, having thrown away old bodies goes to new ones. Weapons do not cut him; fire does not burn him; waters do not wet him; the wind does not dry him away . . ."

This point being clear the Teacher goes on to the next. He says in verse ii 39 that what he has given is knowledge, based upon his own supersensuous experience as well as that of ancient Teachers, but now he wants Arjuna to take up something more than mere knowledge-yoga—he wants him to take up *buddhi-yoga*. *Buddhi* is wisdom, which comes from doing all things for the benefit of souls, not bodies primarily. It is *buddhi* or wisdom to revalue everything from that standpoint.

It is easy to see that the heart of wisdom is love for the co-souls, which Krishna calls indestructible *jivabhutas*, that is, living beings, as distinguished from temporary states and conditions, which are called *bhavas*. Thus the human personalities, in all their varieties are *bhavas*, or existent conditions, but the real men who are owners of the personalities are immortal beings. The lesson that the heart of wisdom is love—goodwill, brotherhood—is driven home by Shri Krishna in his third discourse or chapter, in which he states that the interdependence of all the living beings in the world is universal, and as this is so one should co-operate heartily, not merely mentally but with love, for the very simple reason that the man who loves cannot abstain from activity. He is in a vigorous state, for love is the great energy of the soul. He is like the typical gentleman of Confucius, who was defined as never neutral, but always impartial.

The man of love looks out upon the world, and feels that he must do what he can, however small the opportunity, for the welfare of mankind. This important fact was also soon placed before Arjuna by his Teacher. After pointing out how all the living beings in the world are related to one another in service, how everywhere there is interdependence, he then declared that the man who on earth does not follow the wheel thus revolving lives in vain. Said Shri Krishna: "The man who performs actions without personal attachment reaches the 'beyond'; therefore always do work which ought to be done, without personal attachment. Janaka and others attained perfection through work, so, having regard to the welfare of the world, it is proper for you to work." There is great significance in the words which have been translated "the welfare of the world." They are *loka-sangraha*, *loka* means the inhabitants; *sangraha* means their holding or combining together, their living in harmony. This means love, and if there must be fighting, it is a regrettable necessity, and is to be done still with love in the heart.

It is in this activity that work and love are brought together. What is called *karma-yoga* thus comes into being. Mere work or karma is not yoga, but when that work is energized by love for mankind, it becomes a yoga, that is, a method for the realization of the unity of life. So *karma-yoga* is one branch of Krishna's great teaching of love. The *karma-yogi* "goes about doing good."

And yet that *karma-yoga* is also devotion to God. Among Krishna's devotees, as among those of Christ, there are two distinct kinds. There are those who admire the teacher because he was the great lover of mankind; and there are those who fall down in admiration and devotion before the greatness and goodness of the teacher, and then learn from his example and precept to spread some of his love around them, among their fellow-men. Some love man first and God afterwards; others love God first and man afterwards. The first are the *karma-yogis*; the second the *bhakti-yogis*.

God himself is depicted in the *Gita* as the greatest karma yogi, the pattern for all who would follow that path. He says: "There is nothing in the three worlds, O Partha, that I ought to do, and nothing attainable unattained, yet I engage in work. Certainly if I did not always engage in work without laziness, people on all sides would follow my path. These worlds would become lost if I did not work; I would be the maker of confusion, and would ruin these creatures." No reason can be given why he should thus work, except that he loves the world.

But let no man be discouraged in this work because he himself is small. Let not his vision of great things and devotion to great beings cause him to sink down disconsolate, thinking, "There is nothing that I can do that is big enough to be worth the doing." Let him remember that spiritual things are not measured by quantity but their greatness consists in the purity of their motive. It is the love that counts— not the action. It is one of the greatest glories of this universe that the common and inconspicuous life of ordinary men contains a thousand daily opportunities of spiritual splendor. Says Shri Krishna: "Men reach perfection, each being engaged in his own *karma*. Better is one's own *dharma* though inglorious, than the well-performed *dharma* of another. He who does the duty determined by his own state incurs no fault. By worshipping in his own *karma* (work) him from whom all beings come, him by whom all this is spread out, a man attains perfection."

The words *dharma* and *karma* here require explanation. *Dharma* means where you stand. Each man has to some extent unfolded the flower of his possibility. He stands in a definite position, or holds definite powers of character. It is better that he should recognize his position and be content with it, true to the best he knows, than that he should try to stand in the position of another, or waste his powers in mere envious admiration. To use his powers in the kind of work he can do, upon and with the material that his past karma has provided for him in the present is not only the height of practical wisdom—it is worship of God as well. All life lived in this way is worship; ploughing and reaping, selling and buying—whatever it may be. Conventional forms of kneeling and prostration are not the sole or even the necessary constituents of worship, but every act of the *karma-yogi* and of the *bhakti-yogi* is that. The word bhakti does in fact contain more of the meaning of service than of feeling.

The Lord does not ask from his devotees great gifts. Says Shri Krishna: "When anyone offers to me with devotion a leaf, a flower, a fruit or a little water, I accept that, which is brought with devotion by the striving soul. When you do anything, eat anything, sacrifice anything, give anything or make an effort, do it as an offering to me. Thus shall you be released from the bonds of karma, having their good and bad results, and being free and united through *sannyasa* (renunciation) you will come to me. I am alike to all beings; none is disliked by me, and none is favorite; but those who worship me with devotion are in me and I also am in them. Even if a great evildoer worships me, not devoted to anything else, he must be considered good, for he has determined well. Quickly he becomes a man of *dharma* and attains constant peace." It is clear, then, that this yoga is a way of thinking, and acting, inspired by love, which releases a man from bondage to his own personality.

As there is community of work between God and man, so is there community of interest, and indeed, community of feeling. "All this is threaded on me," says the Divine, "like a collection of pearls on a string." And the reward of the path of yoga is the full realization of this unity: "At the end of many lives the man having wisdom approaches me. By devotion he understands me, according to what I really am; then, having truly known me, he enters that (state) immediately. Although always doing work, having me for goal, through my grace he obtains the eternal indestructible goal."

The love of man for God is more than reciprocated; "He who has no dislike for any being, but is friendly and kind, without greed or egotism, the same in pleasure and pain, forgiving, always content, harmonious, self-controlled and resolute, with thought and affection intent upon me, he, my devotee, is dear to me. He from whom people are not repelled, and who does not avoid the world, free from the agitations of delight, impatience and fear, is dear to me. Those devotees who are intent upon this deathless way of life, thus declared, full of faith, with me as (their) supreme—they are above all dear to me."

Some of the devotional verses suggest a great absence of self-reliance *if* they are taken out of their general context, as, for instance: "Giving up all *dharmas* come only to me as your refuge. Do not sorrow; I will release you from all sins." This "I" to whom reference is so often made, is the one Self, the one life, and therefore it advocates the giving up of selfishness and taking interest in the welfare of all. There is in all this no suggestion anywhere that man should lean upon an external God, an entity. This devotion is required to the "me" which is *all* life, and not a portion of life in some external form, however grand. Shri Krishna speaks for that one life "equally present in all."

The objective side of this is by no means ignored in this teaching of the importance of the soul, indeed, of all souls. While the souls bring themselves more and more into harmony through the power of love or wisdom or *buddhi*, certain material standards are recognized. The material side, consisting of all the *bhavas* or conditions, must be brought into a state of orderliness and appropriateness called *sattwa*. In the teaching of this part of the subject Shri Krishna says that everything in Nature can be classed under one of three heads—it is *tamasic*, that is, material and sluggish, or *rajasic*, that is, active and restless, or *sattwic*, orderly and harmonious. This is in agreement with both ancient and modern thought.

Modern science recognizes three properties in Nature, or three essential constituents in the objectivity of the external world. One of these is materiality, or the ability of something to occupy space and resist the intrusion of another body into the same space. The second is natural energy or force, and the third is natural law and order. There is no object to be found anywhere, be it large or small, which does not show something of all these three, as it occupies space, shows internal or external energy, and "obeys" (or operates) at least some of Nature's laws. These three qualities of Nature were also well known to the ancient Hindus under the names of *tamas*, *rajas* and *sattwa*, and they held that things differed from one another according to the varied proportions of these three ultimate ingredients. Thus an object in which materiality predominated would be described as *tamasic*, and one in which energy was most prominent would be spoken of as *rajasic*.

The same adjectives are applied very fully in the *Gita* to the personalities of men. In the early stages of human awakening we have the very material or *tamasic* man, who is sluggish and scarcely cares to move, unless he is stirred by a strong stimulus from the outside. Next comes the man in whom *rajas* has developed, who is now eager for excitement and full of energy. Perhaps the bulk of people in the modern world are in this condition, or beginning to come into it. *Rajas* sends them forth into great activity with every kind of greed, from the lowest lust of the body to the highest forms of ambition for wealth and fame and power. Men of this kind cannot restrain themselves — to want is to act.

Thirdly come the people who recognize that there is such a thing as natural law, who realize, for example, that it does not pay to eat and drink just what they like and as much as they like, but that there are certain regulations, about kind and quantity and time, which pertain to eating and drinking, and that violation of these regulations leads to pain. In time that pain draws attention to what is wrong and the man begins to use his intelligence, first to try to thwart the pain and avert the law, but later on to understand the law, and obey. And then, in that obedience he learns that life is far richer than ever he thought it to be before, that there is in it a sweet strong rhythm unknown to the man of passion, and that alliance with the law can strengthen and enhance human life beyond all the hopes of the impassioned imagination. All good, thoughtful people are in this third stage, obedient and orderly, and they deserve the name of *sattwic* people.

The disciple has to see that his material and personal life or *bhava* is kept in the *sattwic* condition, as regards body, emotions and thoughts. This is a great yoga undertaking. In this there is plenty to do resembling Patanjali's first five steps. At the same time the disciple must go further than the ordinary good man; he must hold himself above all the qualities of Nature (*tamas*, *rajas* and *sattwa*), *using* the *bhava*, not being immersed and lost in it. "Be thou above the three attributes of Nature, O Arjuna," says the Teacher, "without the pairs of opposites (such as heat and cold, praise and blame, riches and poverty), always steadfast in *sattwa*, careless of possessions, having the (real) self."

These laws work out in a multitude of ways in life, but there are three main principles behind them all—principles of the evolution of consciousness. They express themselves in the powers of will, love and thought, creative in the world, and self-creative in the man. There are only three things that the man must now not do. He must never cease to use his will in work. In that work he must never break the law of love. And in that work of love he must never act; without using his intelligence. These are *principles*—greater than all rules and regulations, because they are the living law of the true self; and not much consideration is required to see that he who follows this law must necessarily show in his practical life all the virtues that are admired by good men of every religion. Indeed, we can adopt from the Greeks the three eternal valuables—goodness, truth and beauty—and say that a man is truly a man only when he is operating these.

These teachings condense down to three practical exercises, which convert experience into soul-knowledge. Shri Krishna does not value life for its own sake, or even brotherhood for its own sake, or even love for its own sake. All actions are valuable only because they lead to knowledge of realities of the soul and the ultimate self. Regarding the aspirant's work or living in the world as stimulating a hunger for something better, which, did he but know it, causes the awakening in himself of a deeper knowledge, and regarding all *buddhi-yoga* and *karma-yoga* as an offering on the altar of world-welfare, valuable also because they are a means of true self-education, useful to everybody, Shri Krishna says: "Better than the offering of any material object is the offering of knowledge, for all work culminates in knowledge. You should learn this by reverence, enquiry and service, and those who know and see the truth will teach you the knowledge. By this you will see all beings without exception in the self, and thus in me. Even if you were the most wicked of evildoers, you would cross over all sin by the raft of (this) knowledge. As fire reduces fuel to ashes, so does the fire of knowledge reduce all *karmas* to ashes. There is indeed no purifier in the world like knowledge. He who is accomplished finds the same in the self in course of time. Having attained (this) knowledge he very soon goes to the peace of the Beyond." The word "knowledge" (*jnana*) in the *Gita* means always something known—high or low. "Wisdom" is *buddhi,* meaning the faculty of understanding the life side of the world.

This passage introduces us to a portion of the definite path of training—the equivalent of Patanjali's practical yoga. It was not sufficient for Arjuna to have great love. If he would tread the path, he must express it in work in the form of service, and must also have an enquiring mind, so as to gain some understanding. The unbalanced character is unfit for the higher path, no matter how great the progress it may have made along one line. Three practices are prescribed; reverence, enquiry and service—in the original, *pranipata, pariprashna* and *seva.* The first means bowing, or respect for the Divine in all beings and events, which is the same thing as Patanjali's *ishwara-pranidhana.* The second is enquiry or questioning, resembling Patanjali's *swadhyaya.* The third is service, another form of practical effort, the equivalent on this path of Patanjali's *tapas*. The requirements are thus the same in each school, but the order and emphasis varies.

When speaking of service, it is necessary to emphasize broad conceptions. Some would narrow it down to personal service to a particular teacher, but the whole *Gita* points to that brotherhood which is the doing of one's best duty to all around, in one's own limited sphere of circumstances and ability. The aspirant should desire the welfare of the world. This does not imply that we should merely engage ourselves with those who are in need, who are weak or poor or ignorant, and bestow our assistance upon them. That is a dangerous pastime, as it tends to a habit of superiority, and often ends in the production of a missionary spirit which is fatal to occult progress. Right association with those who are approximately one's equals is, on the whole, the best means for rendering the greatest help to others and oneself. Life does not flow harmoniously across big gaps. The beginner does not become an expert tennis player by playing against great experts, but with those just a little better than himself, and it is not the business of the greatest expert to teach the mere beginner, just as it is not the business of the chief professor of a college to teach the infant class. A good, sensible, brotherly life, in which one does not embarrass others by making conspicuous sacrifices on their behalf, is always the best. The teaching does not ask for *rajasic* efforts, but a *sattwic* fitting in of oneself into the social welfare.

We may see all mankind in process of evolution or self-unfoldment in seven degrees or stages, according to Shri Krishna's teaching. In the first three stages the man's life is energized from the personality; in the last three, from the real self. In the middle stage there is a conflict between the two, while the man is beginning to work at the three practices mentioned above.

There is one term which Shri Krishna applies to all those who are renouncing allegiance to mere pleasures and self-satisfactions and personal attachment to the objects of the world. He calls them *sannyasis*. In the final discourse of the *Gita*, the eighteenth chapter, there is a long explanation of the meaning of the term *sannyasa*. It is compared with another—*tyaga*. *Tyaga* means abandoning, giving up, leaving behind, and a *tyagi* is therefore one who has renounced the world, given up all possessions, and taken to the uncertain life of a religious mendicant, except perhaps that the term mendicant is not quite appropriate, since this man does not positively beg. *Sannyasa* is the same thing in *spirit*. The *sannyasi* does not necessarily give up the material things, but he gives up personal attachment to them. There is still plenty to do for the man who is becoming more and more conscious of the life around him, and therefore less liable to merely personal interests and motives. The things that he must do are described by Shri Krishna as follows: "Acts of *yajna, dana* and *tapas* should not be given up, but should be done without personal attachment or desire for results." These three kinds of action which alone the *sannyasi* is permitted to do, and which in fact he must do, are sacrifice, gift and effort.

It is always unsatisfactory to try to translate these technical Sanskrit words into one-word equivalents in English. Sacrifice (*yajna*) does not mean the mere surrender of things, but it really means to make all things holy. This occurs when they are offerings. Any action done with an unselfish motive is thus holy. The *sannyasi* does not, however, need to make any ceremonial offerings, because he sees the one life everywhere, and all his actions are direct service of that life. In the West it is significant that "holy" is connected with "whole," and so what is done not for selfish gain but in the interests of all is holy. Sacrifice is thus a law by which living beings are related into one great brotherhood. A very important part of the teaching of the *Gita* is that one should recognize, accept and like the great fact of the mutual support of all living beings, and act or live accordingly. This is called the law of sacrifice.

The *sannyasi* gives freely; leaving it to the law to repay. He also consents to receive only freely, and should any one offer food or anything else for his use, he declines it if the gift is not sincere and free from any suggestion of obligation. His life is one of giving (*dana*). All his powers are completely at the service of mankind. And he must strive also, by *tapas*, to increase those powers. There is plenty to do for the man whose life is only sacrifice, gift and effort, whether he be a wandering monk in India or a railroad magnate in the United States.

This yoga does not exclude meditation. On the contrary it recommends it, but we need not study that here as it has been so fully dealt with in our previous chapters.

In all this teaching one seems to hear the echo of the words of all the spiritual guides of mankind: "We are not interested in the outer man, but in the real man in you. Cling to the real man. That is union with yoga. Let this be a matter for frequent reflection and all else will be purified." The practice of this meditation is essential, but only brings its effect in combination with the practice of true valuation of things in our material living—which is estimation of their value by love, their value *for* somebody. This love leads on to spiritual insight which, as it combines knowing and being, can be called unification—through purification—with the ever present Divine reality.

CHAPTER 3

SHANKARACHARYA'S GNYANA-YOGA

This Teacher, who founded monasteries in India for the study of Vedanta philosophy, is believed by many of his followers to have lived several centuries before Christ, though other scholars place him much later. The date does not matter to us today, but his philosophy does, for it is regarded by some millions of people, and especially by the intellectuals, as the very pinnacle of Aryan thought. It was not that he originated a new philosophy, though he did propound a self-culture or discipline necessary to the understanding of it.

Shankaracharya expounded with great clarity and completeness the already existing philosophy of the Upanishads—a section of the Vedas often called the Vedanta, or end of the Veda, containing the "last word" or highest teaching about the nature of Brahman (God), man and the world. This teaching summed up its conclusions in a number of Great

Sayings, including "There is one reality, but the intellectual persons speak of it variously," "All this certainly is Brahman," "*That* is the reality," "*That, thou art*" and other similar sentences to be (1) listened to, (2) thought about and (3) meditated upon, for the attainment of knowledge of the deepest truth, the very secret of life, the discovery which reveals the unalloyed freedom and happiness of our true self, when false ideas are put aside.

Gnyana or *Jnana* is knowledge. The central doctrine of this philosophy is that everything is one, and it can be known. But that knowing is only by being. We know ourselves not by words but by being ourselves, do we not? And this is happiness, for it seems that though this consciousness of self that we find ourselves to be is troubled, we always ascribe that trouble to something else—something outside—which restricts or annoys us. Who is there who blames himself for his sorrow? Even the thoughtful person who calls himself imperfect ascribes his troubles and sorrows to the imperfections, and says that if he could be without them he would be happy. Generally he tries to get rid of them. So it is by the study of the self that this philosophy proceeds to disclose the occult or secret truth which removes the imperfections and leaves the self free and joyous. Shankaracharya says in one word what all these imperfections are, what it is that we suffer from—it is ignorance, *avidya*. It will be, then, the very height of practical occultism to dispel that ignorance. Because of wrong assumptions we make mistakes, even with the best of intentions—even the intentions are imperfect because of ignorance. So thoughts, intentions and actions are all clouded by ignorance. Finally, even actions are tremendously confused, and without power, because of ignorance.

This is true occultism, then—the dissolution of ignorance at its source, not any small potterings for the gaining of petty pleasures or for the removal of petty pains, but to look behind the veil and find the pure self and no longer play about in the fields of ignorance. This is the real business of life, the Upanishads assert, which can be done, and has been done by successful human beings, who have seen the error and mastered it. At the very least it is better not to walk into new trouble than to busy oneself merely with removing the old.

First of all, Shankaracharya makes a distinction between people who want to *have* and those who want to *know*. To have is connected with external things. The whole world consists of things to have. Shankara does not deny the infinity of worlds or the existence of "higher planes," containing lofty and glorious beings or gods, or that by desiring things of higher planes or heavens and by worshipping the gods people may obtain centuries and even millennia of delight in various lofty heavens; but he affirms that all those things are the playthings of children or the tinsel of fools, who are making them all for themselves because they have not thought about the eternal realities.

He therefore draws a decided distinction between *dharma-jignasa* (the desire to know what should be done in order to obtain better conditions on earth and in heaven) and *Brahma-jignasa* (the desire to know that which is eternal). This is discussed very decisively in Shankara's commentary on the first of the *Brahma-Sutras* or aphorisms. The desire for the "heavens" must be preceded by sense-experience, and confidence in the Vedas, which declare that the heavens exist; but the desire for Brahman must be preceded by thought, thought and more thought (*vichara*), especially with reference to an understanding of the distinction (*viveka*) between the eternal (*nitya*) and temporary (*anitya*) realities. In emphasizing thought, however, Shankara does not leave out study of the Vedanta, which contains much information and advice about seeking the eternal. Shankara's emphasis on thinking is very clear in his *Aparokshanubhuti*: "Thinking should be done for the sake of attaining knowledge of the Self. Knowledge is not attained by any means other than thinking, just as objects are never seen without light. 'Who am I?' 'How is this world produced?' 'Who made it?' and 'What is the material?'—such is the enquiry."

It is well known that we do not see things as they really are, because of our limited point of view, and yet there is in us the craving for greater understanding, because the human soul is one with the divine or universal soul. Each one of us reflects that, just as the disc of the sun may be reflected in many little pools of water. We have thus a dual nature, and though the lower may be satisfied, still the higher makes its claim in a ceaseless desire to understand. If human power and love were to grow so great, as to make our life on earth a perfect paradise of peace and plenty for all, still men would say, "Now, we want to know why all this is so." There are the needs of the personality—food, clothing and shelter, amusement and education, exercise and rest—but beyond these there are spiritual needs, and among them is the real hunger for understanding.

It is not supposed by Shankara that the average or ordinary man can think straight in these matters. He prescribes a course of what may be called purification as a preparation. This is called the *sadhanachatushtayam*, the "group of four accomplishments. They present three departments of self-training, and a concluding condition of mind, as will be seen in the following table:

NAME OF ACCOMPLISHMENT		Function involved
In Sanskrit	*In English*	
1. Viveka	Discrimination	Thought
2. Vairagya	Non-attachment	Feelings
3. Shatsampatti	Six Successes	The Will
4.Mumukshatwa	The State of Longing for Liberation	

Viveka is the practice of discrimination between the fleeting and the permanent. This is the first of three preliminary yogas in this school. It is here that the thinking, thinking, thinking, begins. It is to be applied to oneself, to others and to the whole business of life. It is an inspection of the contents of one's ordinary self, to discriminate between the relatively temporary and permanent. First one may dwell upon the body and realize that it is only an instrument for the conscious self to play upon. Then, one may dwell on the habits of feeling and emotion which have been accumulated during the present lifetime (or, strictly, body-time), and realize these also to be part of the instrument—"I am surely not my feelings and emotions towards things and people." Thirdly, one must meditate upon the fact that the lower mind, the collection of information, ideas and opinions that one has acquired up to this period, is also not the self, but merely an internal library more or less imperfectly indexed, in which the books have a tendency to open at certain places because they have been opened there many times before.

This meditation may then be applied to other people, so that one comes to think of them as the consciousness beyond the personality, and in dealing with them to assist and further the higher purposes of the Self within them rather than the desires rising from the personality. Being a material thing, even up to the mental plane, that personality has its own quality of inertia, and dislikes the discomfort involved in new thinking and willing and feeling, until it is well trained and learns to rejoice in the sharing of a life more than its own. But we must also help to bring the day of triumph nearer for all whom we contact, as Shri Shankaracharya did, for he was one of the world's busiest men.

This meditation must be extended still further to all the business of life, to the family, the shop, the field, the office, society. All these things must be considered as of importance not as they minister to the laziness, selfishness or thoughtlessness of the personality, but as they bear on the advancement in power of will, love and thought of the evolving consciousness in all concerned. It will be seen that works and their objects pass away, but the faculty and ability gained by them remains in the man.

Fifteen to thirty minutes of this kind of meditation

each day is sufficient to establish very soon an entirely new outlook in the personality. Emerson speaks of something of the same kind in his essay on "Inspiration," as the way to an altogether richer life than any of us can possibly reach without it. It can often be practiced to some extent under unfavorable conditions, as for example in the railway train, if one makes up one's mind to take the various disturbances of it with a sweet temper, and lend oneself to the rhythm of its noise.

The second requirement is *vairagya*, an emotional condition in which one does not respond at once to impressions coming from the outer world, but first submits the matter to the discriminative power rising from viveka. If you strike an ordinary man, he will get hot and strike back, or run away, or do something else spontaneous and scarcely rational; but a man having *vairagya* would use his spiritual intelligence before responding. The literal meaning of the word *vairagya* is "absence of color," and in this connection it means absence of passion. *Raga* is coloring, especially redness. People everywhere take their emotional coloring from their environment, according to well known psychological laws; like pieces of glass placed on blue or red or green paper, they change their color. Likes and dislikes rise up in them without reason, at the mere sight of various objects, and the appearance of different persons calls up pride, anger, fear and other personal emotions.

They are constantly judging things not with their intelligence but by their feelings and emotional habits. "This is good, that is bad," means generally nothing more than, "I like this; I do not like that." A man dislikes a thing because it disturbs his physical or emotional convenience or his comfortable convictions, "I thought I had done with thinking about that—take it away, confound you," grumbles the man comfortably settled in his opinions, as in a big armchair.

Vairagya is the absence of agitation due to things outside. A mistaken idea which is sometimes associated with this word is that it implies absence of emotion. That is not so. The purified personality responds to the higher emotions, the love emotions that belong to the real self. Those emotions come from that aspect of the indwelling consciousness which feels other lives to be as interesting as one's own. This is the root of all the love emotions— admiration, kindness, friendship, devotion and others—which must not be confused with any sort of passion, which is personal or bodily desire. If a man has *vairagya* and he is still at all emotional, his emotion must express some form of love.

Vairagya may be developed by a form of meditation in which the aspirant should picture and turn over in mind the various things that have been causing him agitation, or the disturbing emotions of pride, anger and fear. Having made a picture of the cat spilling the ink on the best tablecloth, or of your enemy putting in a bad word for you with your employer or superior behind your back, you calmly look at it, meditate on it, and the light of your own intelligence will see the real value of the experience and this removal of ignorance will also remove the agitating emotion. This is a question of feeling, not of action. Do not here substitute the deadly coldness that some people sometimes feel instead of anger, and imagine that to be the calm state.

The calmness obtained in this way will soon make all the other meditation far more effective than before, because meditation best opens the door to the inner world and all its inspiration when the body is quiet, the emotions are calm, and the attention is turned to the subject of thought without any muscular or nervous strain or physical sensation whatever. Incidentally it should be said that meditation with physical sensation or strain may prove injurious to health, but meditation rightly done in this way can never do the least harm.

The third requirement is called *shatsampatti*, which may be translated "the six forms of success." The will is now used to make all conditions favorable for the further development of *viveka*. To understand the function of the will, it is necessary to realize that it is the faculty with which we change *ourselves*. Thought is *kriyashakti*, the power of mind that acts upon matter; but it is the will with which we change our thoughts and other inward conditions. Now will-power is to be used to bring the whole life of the man within the purpose of *jnana-yoga*. This work is the equivalent of the *tapas* of Patanjali and the *seva* of Shri Krishna.

The six forms of success are: (1) *shama*, control of mind, (2) *dama*, control of body; (3) *uparati*, which means cessation from eagerness to have certain persons and things around one, and therefore a willing acceptance of what the world offers— contentment with regard to things and tolerance with regard to persons, a glad acceptance of the material available for a life's work. The fourth is *titiksha*, patience, the cheerful endurance of trying conditions and the sequence of karma. The fifth is *shraddha*, fidelity and sincerity, and therefore confidence in oneself and others. The sixth is samadhana, steadiness, with all the forces gathered together and turned to the definite purpose in hand.

Every one of these six practices shows the will at work producing that calm strength which is its own special characteristic. This is necessary for yoga, and anything in the nature of fuss or push, or excitement is against it. In no case does this calmness mean the reduction of activity or work, but always that the work is done with greater strength but less noise.

Success is marked by quietness, the best indication of power. Thus the mind and body will be active but calm; and there will be contentment, patience, sincerity and steadiness.

The three branches of training already mentioned make the entire personality exceedingly sensitive to the higher self, so that a great longing arises for a fuller measure of realization. This is called *mumukshatwa*, eagerness for liberation.

To complete this occult knowledge one must combine the *maya* doctrine with the self-realization doctrine. It is, of course, the self-realization of itself that is the full achievement. And since *maya* does not mean something unreal but something outside the categories of both the real and unreal, and is in fact nothing but error, we shall have to say that the power of *maya* is a power of the self itself, and that all that is not unreal in the *maya* is beyond time and space, a part of the self itself, whatever "parts" may mean-in the indivisible. The general dictum of all the yogas is fulfilled here—that never will the yogi find something that could be anticipated, but only something unknown before, which, however, by universal testimony, is true being, pure consciousness and incredible joy. All the explanations given in this chapter and much more will be found in my book on Vedanta entitled *The Glorious Presence*.

It will be useful now to see that the same three means of self-guidance are employed in all the three schools we have studied so far—of Patanjali, of Shri Krishna and of Shankaracharya. It becomes obvious when we thus compare them that all are aiming at maturity of mind, the ripening of the three functions of will, love and thought. They put these three in different order, however, indicating the different temperaments of those who take to the different schools of occult practice and thought. The following table will make the comparison clear.

Patanjali	*Krishna*	*Shankara*
1. *Tapas* (Will)	1. *Pranipata* (Love)	1. *Viveka* (Thought)
2. *Swadhyaya* (Thought)	2. *Pariprashna* (Thought)	2. *Vairagya* (Love)
3. *Ishwara-pranidhana* (Love)	3. *Seva* (Will)	3. *Shatsampatti* (Will)

When the student has followed this preliminary training with some success he will be ready for two things (1) the understanding of the doctrine of *maya*, and (2) the direct visioning of the Self.

Maya has often been translated "illusion," whence it has been thought that Shankara teaches that all this world does not exist, and people only imagine that it does so—that there is nothing there. That is not so. He does not deny the existence of objects, but affirms that we see them wrongly—just as a man may see a piece of rope on the ground and mistake it for a snake, or as he may see a post in the distance and think it to be a man.

It is necessary to know that *maya* has two functions: "covering-up" (*avarana*) and "throwing-out" (*vikshepa*). The first is declared to be the effect of *tamas*, which hides or obstructs the life, and the second the result of *rajas,* or energy. "Covering-up" implies that although we are—every one—universal in our essential nature, our attention is now given to less than the whole. Most of the reality is covered up, and since we see only the remainder, it must necessarily become unsatisfying and stupid and even painful, when we have played with it long enough to exhaust its lessons for us. When we have read a book and absorbed the ideas in it, we do not want to read it again. If it is forced upon us, the experience will be painful. We may laugh at a good joke told by a friend to-day, but if he persists in telling us the same story again and again it will be far from a joke. Our life must be moving on, and overcoming the *avarana*; there is no long-lasting pleasure or gain in standing still on any platform of knowledge that we may have gained at any time or stage.

"Covering-up" does not mean that objects of experience lack reality. The *maya* or illusion is that we do not see their *full* reality; we see too little, not too much. So far as they go they have an excellent flavor of reality, but their incompleteness is unsatisfying.

The second function of *maya*, "throwing-out" (*vikshepa*), means that we put forth our thought and energy in reference to that part of reality which for us individually has not been covered up, and thereby we produce the world of *maya* or created things, which are only temporary (*anitya*).

The power of "throwing-out" is not merely of the mind, but is actually creative, and this it is which produces all the *forms* around us, the world of manifestation. The objects therein are very much like pictures painted by an artist. They represent his expression of such part of the reality as is not covered up. As he looks at the picture and realizes how defective and even nonsensical it is, the hunger arises in him for something more satisfying, which then works at removing the "covering-up." Thereby arises what is called intuition, which always comes as the result of a complete study of any fact or group of facts in the world of experience. It is in this manner that experience is educative. It gives us nothing from the outside, but enables us to introduce ourselves to a fuller part of reality. So *avarana* resembles concentration, and the result of experience can be compared to contemplation. Thus *maya*, while not reality, is also not unreality.

Shankara speaks in very strong language about the effect of *avarana* and *vikshepa* in practical life: "The function of *avarana*, made of *tamas*, covers up the shining Self, which has unlimited faculties, just as the shadow of the moon hides the disc of the sun. When there is thus the obscuration of a man's real and stainlessly radiant Self, he thinks he is the body, which is not the Self. Then the great power of *rajas* called *vikshepa* afflicts him by the binding qualities of passion, anger, etc., so that this unintelligent man, deprived of real knowledge of the Self, through being swallowed by the crocodile of the great delusion, wanders about, rising and falling in the ocean of limited existence. As clouds produced by the sun obscure the sun as they develop, so does egotism arising from the Self obscure the Self as it flourishes. And as on a bad day when thick clouds swallow the sun, and they also are afflicted by sharp cold winds, so does the power of acute *vikshepa* annoy the man of confused intelligence with many troubles. By these two powers the man is bound; deluded by them he wanders about, thinking the body to be himself."

Then comes the question how to remove these two: "Unless the *avarana* function ceases completely, vikshepa cannot be conquered. When subject and object are separated, like milk from water, then *avarana* disappears on its own account in the Self. Perfect discrimination, arising from clear perception, having distinguished the subject and the object, cuts

away the bondage of delusion made by *maya*, and then for the free man there is no more wandering about."

The substance of material things is called *sat*, or being. Consciousness, with its powers of will, love and thought, is called *chit*. Beyond those three aspects of consciousness is *ananda*, the true life that is sheer happiness. The being of true life is happiness. First a man must get over the delusion that he *is* the body, and realize that he is consciousness using the body. He *has* a body. Then, later on, he must realize that he *is not* the powers of consciousness, but that he simply *uses* these. Then he will be his own true self, *ananda*, happiness, which is the nature of our pure being. But that happiness is one with consciousness (*chit*) and being (*sat*), as the man will find on reaching illumination; so the world of sat is real, part of his own true life, and not illusion. *Maya* was the practical effect of the mistake (*avidya*) by which he confused together, first consciousness and external being, and then consciousness and his psychological or internal being.

The analogy of dreaming is employed to illustrate these points. Just as on waking we realize that our dream was irrational, so on waking from the dream that we now call waking we shall realize the truth that will make our present outlook appear irrational.

Not that it is irrational, but that the true vision has the correct data or perception. Even our present knowledge, it is said, is ignorance, or better un-wisdom, because we are always looking at things with the eyes of the flesh, while we ought to look at them with the eyes of the spirit, that is, from the standpoint of the imperishable consciousness.

The question then arises—what is the best practical way to attain reality. To this two answers may be given: (1) Realize the infinite possibilities of every finite experience, and (2) do not mix yourself with your objects of experience. As to the first, it means simply that we can learn from one thing what we can learn from many things. For example, a man has one mother. If he has learnt to love that mother, then he is predisposed to love any mother whom he may meet. He does not need to learn the lesson all over again in connection with those other mothers. As instructed in the *Gita*, by attending to his own experience a man reaches perfection.

Another instance of the same principle is the use of the human body. If we had to attain some kind of perfection which involved knowledge of all things which people are making for themselves by their "throwing-out," this body would not be enough. In such a case we should need seven-league boots and a hundred or a thousand arms and legs instead of only two of each. But this is not the way of the evolution of life. It can reach its perfection through an ordinary body with two arms and two legs. It need not have the muscular system of a professional athlete or the mental capacity of a German chemist or lexicographer. Realize the infinite possibilities of the moment's experience, cease to resent any of the experience, and immediately most of the pain and sorrow that it may contain is emptied out of it, and it becomes immensely fruitful.

There are two ways in which we may live our lives amidst events of the world, without retiring at all from that world. In both cases the mixing with the world will be the same, but in one there is real confusion (that is, fusing together) and in the other merely mixing. For example, if milk and water are put together it is very difficult to separate them, but if oil and water are mixed together, although they are together they retain their individuality. So in relation to the world we are to be like oil in water, not milk in water. We must distinguish between "the world," "my world" and "myself"—three things, not two. It is like a person playing a game of chess. The board is there—my world. The pieces have been moved into a certain position. A good player does not become excited and flustered, whether he is winning or losing. He cannot, in fact, really in himself either win or lose. Even if his pieces are captured one by one, if he has played the game to the best of his ability he has developed his faculties, and on the whole he is a little more likely to profit by a lost than by a won game.

These facts being established, people sometimes raise the academic question: "Whence comes this ignorance which hides the full reality?" With regard to this Buddha's advice was: "Sink not the string of thought into the fathomless." The fact is that we have to begin our reasoning and our activity from the place in which we find ourselves. We are apparently on a ladder, which goes upwards out of sight. The important thing is that it goes upwards. But one would not avoid the ultimate question. The answer to it is that space and time are a creation of ignorance—they come into being through the "covering-up," and disappear for us when the covering is removed. How, then, can the questions, "where" and "whence," which ask for an answer in terms of time and space, be applied to this matter? Evidently there is some sort of evolution or unfoldment, but it is not a change in time and space. That this is so is indicated by the unchanging character of our feeling of "I" which is the same point of reference in youth and age, and whether we be here or there, and standing on our heads or on our feet.

The meditations of Shankara are practical, because they are not merely thoughts about things, considered as objects, dwelt upon in the third grammatical person. First, the student must say to himself, "I am not *it*"—"it" being the personality, physical and psychological, composed of body, personal emotions and fixed ideas. This means not simply the set of "vehicles" as they stand, but also their habits of action, emotion and thought—the entire personality. He must put that outside himself. Secondly, he must say, "I am not *you*," referring now to that in himself which he would call "you" in another person—the collection of thinkings, lovings and willings or powers of consciousness. The personality is something that you *use*—not something that you *are*. So also the conscious powers are something that you *use*, not something that you *are*. Thirdly, he must say, "I am I. I can take up and put down these powers of consciousness. I can enlarge or reduce them." But in the second stage he must take care to think of his own ordinary consciousness always as *you*, never as *it*, nor as *I*, otherwise he will remain in the *you*, and not reach the *I*.

All happiness in life is beyond the limited consciousness and is experienced when that activity is forgotten. All the delight that comes from response to beauty, love and truth in the world, and from the powers of will, love and thought in consciousness, lie in the Self beyond, when the world and the limited self are forgotten, and time and space have been swallowed up in something greater, beyond their limitations. Beyond common consciousness, in a state better than that limited consciousness, we are, and all clinging to mental ideas about oneself, pleasurable or not, bars the realization of that truth. That unchanging *I* is *ananda*, happiness, the one reality. To know this directly, not by logic, is the high purpose of the Vedanta.

CHAPTER 4

THE HATHA AND LAYA YOGAS

The practice of *hatha-yoga* is composed chiefly of *pranayama*, which is regulation of breath, *asana*, the practice of various postures, and a set of six *bandhas* or body-purifications. Although the writer of these words holds to the opinion that these physical practices cannot develop the mind at all, or contribute to its yogic or occult experience, he agrees that when the *hatha-yoga* exercises are properly done they are very beneficial to the body. As long as people have bodies they should treat them if possible as prize animals, but if that is too much to ask they should at least give them good exercise as well as good rest and good food. In this sense only one should understand the well-known maxim: "No *raja* without *hatha*; no *hatha* without *raja*."

The *asanas* or postures have some advantages over ordinary physical exercises intended for muscular development. Although these latter do also stimulate good breathing and benefit the nervous system to some extent, especially if used in conjunction with proper relaxation at suitable times, the *hatha-yoga* postures do in addition provide suppleness and slenderness, and give massage to the internal organs. Besides this, when allied to suitable and not excessive breathing exercises, the entire body benefits. None of the yoga schools aims at abnormal strength—a reasonable standard such as is suitable for the ordinary purposes of life is regarded as sufficient, and more than that may often be just a matter of personal satisfaction or pride, not the spiritual attainment which the *hatha-yogis, raja-yogis* and all other yogis are aiming at, which contains no self-satisfaction. Incidentally, one must remark, great mental muscularity—to use a metaphor—is also not sought by any of them. If there are mental giants among them, this must be put down to some work of supererogation in that line in their previous lives.

In an earlier chapter we have spoken of *hatha* as the "sun" and "moon" breaths. It comes in, say some works, with the sound of ha and goes out with the sound of tha. Another explanation is that the "sun" and "moon" correspond to the breaths traveling through the right and left nostrils. Still a third view is that as the whole word *hatha* ordinarily means forcefulness, the system of *hatha-yoga* is one which, at least as compared with other yogas, requires considerable energy. It has already been stated that in those yogas the thinkings and meditations are intended to be done without allowing any tension in the body.

We may introduce the picture of a typical form of *hatha-yoga* breathing by quoting from the *Shiva Sanhita*:

"The wise man, having closed the right nostril with the thumb of the right hand, and having drawn air in through the left nostril, should hold his breath as long as he can, and then let it out through the right nostril slowly and gently. Next, having breathed in through the right nostril, he should retain the air as long as possible, and then breathe it out gently and very slowly through the left nostril.

"Let him thus practice regularly, with twenty retentions, at sunrise, midday, sunset and midnight, every day, keeping a peaceful mind, and in three months the channels of the body will have become purified. This is the first of four stages of *pranayama* (regulation of breath), and the signs of it are that the body becomes healthy and likeable and emits a pleasant odor, and there will be good appetite and digestion, cheerfulness, a good figure, courage, enthusiasm and strength.

"There are, however, certain things which the *swarasadhaka* (breath-practiser) must avoid: foods which are acid, astringent, pungent, salty, mustardy and bitter, and those fried in oil, and various activities of body and mind, bathing before sunrise, stealing, harmfulness, enmity, egotism, cunning, fasting, untruth, cruelty to animals, sexual attachments, fire, much conversation and much eating. On the contrary, he should use and enjoy *ghi* (butter clarified by simmering), milk, sweet food, betel without lime, camphor, a good meditation-chamber with only a small entrance, contentment, willingness to learn, the doing of household duties with *vairagya*, singing of the names of Vishnu, hearing sweet music, firmness, patience, effort, purity, modesty, confidence and helping the teacher. If there is hunger, a little milk and butter may be taken before practice, but there should be no practice for some time after meals. It is better to eat a small amount of food frequently (with at least three hours' intervals) than much at once. If the body perspires it should be well rubbed (with the hands). When the practice has become well established, these rules need not be so strictly observed." [1]

One does not wish to put any of these *hatha-yoga* practices into print, to be read by various kinds of people, without sounding a warning. Many people have brought upon themselves incurable illness and even madness by practising them without providing the proper conditions of body and mind. The old yoga books are full of such warnings, and they tell

---

[1] *Shiva Sanhita* iii 22-40; abridged translation.

the would-be practicer to go to a teacher who really knows all about these things, to receive personal inspection and instruction. For example, the *Gheranda Sanhita* announces that if one begins the practices in hot, cold or rainy weather, disease will be contracted, and also if there is not moderation in diet, for only one half the stomach must ever be filled with solid food. When the present writer tried, as a boy of fourteen or fifteen, the long alternate breathing for three quarters of an hour, he found when he stood up that he had lost his sense of touch and weight. He handled things without feeling them, and walked without any sense of touching the ground. The sense returned only after ten or fifteen minutes.

The *Hatha Yoga Pradipika* states that control of breath must be brought about very gradually, "as lions, elephants and tigers are tamed," or else "the experimenter will be killed," and by any mistake there arises cough, asthma, head, eye and ear pains, and many other diseases. The *Shandilya Upanishad* gives the same warning. On the other hand, right practice may be undertaken by anybody, even the young and the old, the sick and the weak, and will result in slenderness and rightness of body.[2]

The theory behind these breathing exercises is that between the mind and the body comes *prana*. This

---

[2] *Gheranda Sanhita* i 64, and ii 20.

word is translated "principle of life"—referring to life in the body. Five vital airs are mentioned extensively in the Sanskrit literature which touches on the physiology of the human body. *Prana* is always referred to as the chief of these vital airs. The word comes from a verbal root "an" meaning "to breathe," and thus "to live." Patanjali in his aphorism on *Pranayama* calls it regulation of the manner of movement of *shwasa* and *prashwasa*, that is, breathing.[3] The late Dr. Vaman R. Kokatnur, noted scientist and Sanskrit scholar, in a paper read at the American Chemical Society's meeting in Detroit in September 1927, quoted a text which says that what is inhaled is *prana* and what is exhaled is *apana*. On various grounds he made out a good case for these being oxygen and carbon dioxide, a third "air," *udana*, being hydrogen. Of the other two of the five, *samana* is generally spoken of as essential to digestion and *vyana* "pervades the whole body." Many speak of these five airs as being something else, fine or "etheric," but all agree that various ways of breathing affect them all. Many of the teachers recommend the traditional proportions of one unit of time for inbreathing (*puraka*), four units for holding the breath within (*Kumbhaka*), and two units for out-breathing (*rechaka*). The *Shiva Sanhita* speaks of the units being gradually lengthened, as seen in verse iii 57: "When the yogi is able to practice

---

[3] See *Practical Yoga: Ancient and Modern*, by Ernest Wood; Ch. 8, Aphorism ii 49.

77

holding the breath for an hour and a half, various *siddhis* (faculties and powers) arise, including prophecy, traveling at will, sight and hearing at a distance, vision of the invisible worlds, entering others' bodies, turning various metals into gold, invisibility at will, and moving in the air."

Various teachers and books offer more elaborate, as well as some simpler, breathing exercises. The following eight are often mentioned: (1) Practice *kumbhaka* (holding the breath) until the pressure of air is felt from head to foot, then breathe out through the right nostril; (2) breathe in deeply and noisily, hold as before, and exhale through the left nostril; (3) putting the tongue between the lips breathe in with a hissing sound; exhale through both nostrils; (4) breathe out as fully as possible, then in with a hissing sound, and go on very rapidly like bellows, until tired; then exhale by the right, or (5) the left nostril; (6) breathe in with the sound of a female bee; (7) after breathing in, contract the throat, place the chin on the chest; breathe out very slowly; (8) simply hold the breath, without inbreathing or out-breathing, as long as you like.

While issuing warnings about these exercises, I would like to add that many have found benefit from the following simple practice. Breathe in fairly fully while saying mentally to yourself *"puraka;"* hold the breath in without any muscular effort while saying "*kumbhaka, kumbhaka, kumbhaka, kumbhaka;*" breathe out quite fully while saying "*rechaka, rechaka.*" This may be done at odd times as a pick-me-up, with generally about ten repetitions. The best slowness or quickness of the words should be found by the student for himself, but all the words should be of the same length. A tendency to lengthen them a little may gradually and rightly appear.

Some teachers maintain that all the impurities of the body may be removed merely by control of breath, but others hold that it is necessary to practice also certain cleansings, especially in the case of persons who are flabby and phlegmatic.

The six principal purifications are: (1) slowly (under the direction of a teacher) learn to swallow a clean, slightly warm, thin cloth, four fingers broad and fifteen spans long; hold on to the end of it, and gradually draw it out again; (2) take an enema sitting in water and using a small bamboo tube; shake well and dispel; (3) draw a fine thread, twelve fingers long, in at one nostril and out at the mouth; (4) look at something without winking, until tears come; (5) with the head bent down, slowly massage the intestines, round and round both ways, and (6) breathe rapidly, like the bellows of a blacksmith. These acts are said to remove corpulence and many other diseases.

The *Gheranda Sanhita* has a much bigger collection—about twenty-four purifications—which includes swallowing air with the lips formed "like the beak of a crow," and expelling it from below; doing the same with water; gently pressing the intestines towards the spine one hundred times, massaging the depression at the bridge of the nose (especially after waking and after meals); vomiting by tickling the throat; gargling; drawing air softly in at one nostril, and sending it out softly at the other, alternately; drinking water in at the nostrils and letting it out at the mouth.

Closely connected with the elaborate practices of *pranayama* are the postures (*asanas*). Quite often eighty-four of these are enumerated, but the *Shiva Sanhita* contents itself with recommending four, which are called "The Adept Seat," "The Lotus Seat," "The Powerful Seat," and "The Swastika Seat." These are briefly as follows: (1) body straight, legs crossed, one heel at the anus, the other at the front, gaze between the eyebrows, chin on breast; (2) legs folded with feet, soles upwards, on opposite thighs, arms crossed, hands on thighs, tongue pressed against teeth, chin on breast or held up, gaze on tip of nose (or straight in front); or arms may be crossed behind, hands holding great toes; (3) legs stretched out, apart, head held in hands and placed on knees; (4) feet between calves and thighs, body straight. The

Hatha Yoga Pradipika also advocates four *asanas* especially, two being the same and two different.

An excellent modern book on *pranayama, asanas* etc., is *Yoga Asanas* by Swami Shivananda, of Rishikesh, in the Himalayas.[4] In this the Swami explains with illustrations a large number of postures, including the *Sukhasana,* or "pleasant posture" described and recommended for the West in my *Practical Yoga: Ancient and Modern*. He also gives very useful simple breathing exercises as well as the more elaborate ones.

We come now to another school of yoga called the laya yoga. Laya means "latent" or "in suspense." The especial features of this yoga are its study and practice of *kundalini* and the *chakras. Kundalini* is described as a force lying in three and a half coils like a sleeping serpent, in a cavity near the base of the spine. This is regarded as a goddess or power, "luminous as lightning," who, even though sleeping, maintains all living creatures. She lies there with her head blocking a fine channel which goes straight up the spine and is known as the *sushumna*. Some, to link this up with modern thought, have called it the fount of bodily electricity.

---

[4] Published by The Vaman Press, 31 Broadway, Madras, India.

The purpose of the laya-yoga practice is to awaken the *kundalini* (or "coiled one"), who will start up hissing, and can then be carried through the series of six *chakras* (literally, "wheels"), which are threaded upon that channel at various points in the body, which are situated at the level of the base of the spine, the root of the penis, the navel, the heart, the throat and the eyebrows. These *chakras* are depicted somewhat as flowers rather than wheels, and have petals respectively numbering four, six, eight, twelve, sixteen, and two. The works describing these *chakras*, and the effects of meditation upon them or in them, are altogether too numerous even to mention.[5] They are depicted with very much symbology. For example, the *anahata chakra* (at the heart) has a *yantra* or design showing twelve petals, each one bearing a certain letter of the alphabet. In the center circle there is a pair of interlaced triangles, having written in the middle of them the syllable "*yam*" (which is a *mantra* or sound which can produce some effect when properly repeated). This *yam* is pictured as riding on a black antelope, and, in its final sound *m*, which is written as a dot, a figure

---

[5] Except that one would wish to refer the Western reader to *The Serpent Power*, by Arthur Avalon, published by Ganesh and Co., Thyagarayanagar, Madras, India, for very full information.

representing the male divinity is placed. He is styled Isha, has three eyes, and holds out his hands with gestures of dispelling fear and granting boons. Near

by, in the pericarp of the lotus (for the *chakras* are also called lotuses) is the female divinity Kakini, seated on a red lotus, having golden color, dressed in yellow clothes, wearing all kinds of jewels and a garland of bones. She has four arms, two hands bearing a noose and a skull, and the other two showing signs of dispelling fear and granting boons. In the center, above the interlaced triangles, is an inverted triangle as bright as lightning, and in that a symbol of Shiva of a golden color with a crescent moon surmounted by a dot upon its head. This *chakra*, like all the *padmas* (lotus flowers) is brightly colored, the petals and pericarp being red.

One cannot attempt in this brief space to unravel the significance of all these letters, colors and symbols, or to give the symbols of the other five *padmas*. Each *chakra* has its own diagram, colors, animal, divinities, letters, etc. It will be evident that the yogi, as he meditates in each of them in the course of his progress, will have plenty to think about. Arthur Avalon's excellent translation of the *Shatchakra Nirupana*, with comments thereon, is a mine of information on the subject, but the thorough student should also read various minor Upanishads, Puranas and general works on yoga touching on this subject. There is a certain amount of conflicting testimony on the subject of colors, divinities etc., but this does not mar the general unity of information as regards all the main features.

There is in all the literature on the subject a poetical rather than an exact description of what happens as *kundalini* rises. The spine is called "the axis of creation" for the body. In that is the channel *sushumna*; within that another, named *vajroli* and within that again another, called *chitrini*, "as fine as a spider's thread." On this tube the lotuses are said to be threaded "like knots on a bamboo rod." Kundalini rises up little by little, as the yogi employs his will. In one practice he brings her as far as he can, and, as she pierces any one of the lotuses, its face, which was turned downwards before, turns upwards, and when the meditation is finished he leads her back to her home near the base of the spine.[6]

---

[6] There is a little difference of opinion here. Some hold that once she has reached the heart chakra that will be her permanent home, and she will not return below it. Others say that even from the beginning she was at the level of the navel. These are not altogether reasonable views, if, as is usually believed, *kundalini* has the work of purifying and transmuting all the lower centers on her return journey from the higher.

It is further explained that as she leaves each *chakra* on the way up, she withdraws the functions of that center, and so makes them latent, hence the term laya-yoga, or the Yoga of Suspension. It is, of course, natural that in such a process, as attention is given more and more to the higher thought, the lower responses should become latent, as, for example, when we are reading and do not hear or see a person who enters the room.

Kundalini proceeds upwards until she reaches the great "thousand-petalled lotus" at the top of the head, beyond all the six *chakras*. There she enjoys the bliss and power of union with the source of all life, and afterwards, as she returns through the centers she gives back to each its specific powers, purified and enhanced. The process of bringing *kundalini* to the highest point is usually considered to require some years, but there are exceptional cases in which it is done quickly.

The hatha-yoga books take up a curious view of the mind in relation to all these matters. It is expressed in a few verses of the *Hatha-Yoga Pradipika*. "The mind is the lord of the senses; the breath is the lord of the mind; and that depends on *nada*."[7] "There is talk of *laya, laya,* but what is its character? *Laya* is the

---

[7] *Hatha-Yoga Pradipika* iv 29.

non-arising of further vasanas,[8] and the forgetting of external things." [9] Some of the minor Upanishads, such as the *Muktika* of the *Shukla-Yajurveda*, have a similar idea.

Even so brief an account of these practices as this is would be incomplete without mention of the *mudras*, or physical practices, and the *nadas*, or internal sounds. The *mudras*, although in some cases similar to the purifications, are intended for a different purpose—to obtain some delight or power, and to awaken *kundalini*, for it is held that the awakening can take place through *asanas* (postures), *kumbhakas* (holdings of the breath) and *mudras*.

Though there are many *mudras*, only ten are usually recommended. Among the most popular ones intended to awaken *kundalini* is that of supporting the body on the palms of the hands and softly striking the posteriors on the ground, which is also considered to remove wrinkles and grey hair. In another, very highly recommended, the membrane under the tongue is gradually cut ("one hair's breadth every seven days"), and rubbed with salt and turmeric, so that the severed parts will not join. The tongue is also gradually lengthened by a

---

[8] Vasana is the "perfume" of past attachments or desires, which now produce pleasure and pain; if one may use a crude simile, like the smell of onions long after they have been eaten.
[9] *Hatha-Yoga Pradipika* iv 34.

process resembling milking, so that after six months the yogi can turn it upwards into the cavity at the back of the palate, and thus, with the hole closed and the breath suspended, contemplate *kundalini* and "drink the nectar" flowing there. Another physical method requires a sort of massage for an hour and a half morning and evening, for up to forty-five days. Still another requires the feet to be crossed behind the neck.

It must be mentioned that those raja yogis who do not approve of the awakening of *kundalini* by these external methods, nor even by meditation upon it, nevertheless usually believe that *kundalini* naturally awakens and rises as a result of the purely internal meditations which they practice. This takes place a little at a time so that there is no strong feeling or pain in the body, as is often the case when it is done by the *hatha-yoga* methods. The purifying and subliming effects of the return journey through the *chakra* in all cases awakens some degree of clairvoyance and similar powers, but what the yogi sees will depend upon his state of mind, and even then the understanding of what he sees will depend upon his evolutionary status. There is plenty of room for error, inasmuch as his own thoughts and those of others may easily be mistaken for objective realities, as in dreams.

Some of the books prescribe an "elephant *mudra*,"

which is performed by standing up to the neck in water, drinking it in through the nostrils, sending it out through the mouth and then reversing the process. This resembles the action of elephants in the pools and rivers, though they use the trunk only, not the mouth.

Now we come to the *nadas* or sounds. The *Shiva Sanhita* instructs the yogi to close the ears with the thumbs, the eyes with the index fingers, the nostrils with the middle fingers and the lips with the remaining four fingers. After some practice, he will begin to hear the mystic sounds. The first will be like the hum of a bee, then a flute and then a *vina*. With more practice there comes the sound of bells, and afterwards thunder. The mind of the yogi becomes absorbed in these sounds, and he forgets the external things which could distract him.[10] These sounds are usually called *anahata*, or belonging to the heart center. According to the *Hatha Yoga Pradipika*, when the ears, eyes, nose and mouth are closed, a clear sound is heard — first like the tinkling of ornaments, and later like kettle-drums; later still there is the sound of the flute and the *vina*. In the middle stage there may be the sound of bells and horns. The yogi must give his attention to the subtler

---

[10] *Shiva Sanhita* v 22-28. See also *The Voice of the Silence*, by H. P. Blavatsky, which gives the order as like the sounds of the nightingale, silver cymbal, shell, lute, trumpet, thunder, and much other very valuable information on yoga.

sounds. The *Nadabindu Upanishad* also gives much the same order of sounds as the *Hatha Yoga Pradipika,* mentioning in stage one the sound of the sea, clouds, waterfalls and kettledrums, in the second stage that of drums, bells and horns, and thirdly, that of tinkling bells, flutes, *vinas* and bees. The *Hansa Upanishad* gives the order more in agreement with the *Shiva Sanhita.* First come soft chattering sounds, then that of the bell, conch, lute, cymbals, flute, drum, double drum, and, lastly, thunder. The *nada laya* or "absorption through sound" is regarded as a great aid to concentration.

Samadhi, the highest practice of yoga, is conceived in a very material manner in the *hatha-yoga* books. The idea is that the yogi in *samadhi* is uninfluenced by anything external, because the senses have become inactive, and he does not even know himself or others. Although the *Gheranda Sanhita* says that *samadhi* involves union of the individual with the supreme Self (*Paratman*) so that "I am Brahma and no other; Brahma am I, without any sorrows; I am of the nature of fundamental existence, knowledge and bliss, always free and self -supporting," it also prescribes, for the attainment of this, various *mudras* or physical practices, such as that of turning the tongue into the nasal cavity and stopping the breath, the theory being that all you need to do is to cut off contact with this world, and the other state will be there.

89

CHAPTER 5

THE BHAKTI AND MANTRA YOGAS

Bhakti, or devotion, arises from the appreciation of goodness. There will be no devotional feeling towards what is not good. If some persons were to worship or rather propitiate a dangerous deity it would not be devotion. So devotion implies goodness and is towards goodness. It is a form of love, but essentially love of something or some person who is "good."

Merchants, who speak of goods, not of mere things or articles, are in this particular excellent psychologists. Goods are things which are good for us, or we might better put it, good to us. We go further as our intelligence or knowledge increases and recognize that some things which are not good to us are good to others. "The farmer prays for rain, the washerman for sun," says the Japanese proverb. On this basis, everything is seen to be good because everything is good to some being.

When men ask themselves where all these goods come from they easily ascribe them to a goodness which has the nature of a superior mind. They find that the good man is one who positively produces goods of some kind and passes them on to others. Not only the things he produces but he himself is thus a manifestation of goodness. From such thoughts it is easy to pass on to the idea of a deity or deity who is goodness, and, in the height of this idea, is good to all and always, even when the goodness of his gift of the moment is not understood and felt as such. In this way the intellect permits the goodness to be universalized, and prevents the judgment of goodness from being based on one's own personal pleasure or one's own material welfare. Thus devotion, which arises at first from the reception of some goods, ends up by declaring that all is good, and this devotion then makes logical a predisposition towards appreciative feelings, even when there is not understanding.

That is true and complete religious devotion, which never questions but always appreciates everything, or judges all things and their Giver as expressions and sources of that goodness. In the West philosophers have said that it is possible to get good out of every experience, so one should "look for the good in everything"; but in India they always went one better than that by saying one should "look for the God in everything," because in this way the feelings as well as the intellect had their play. In looking for the good in everything there is usually a somewhat antagonistic feeling. This philosopher says he will face all situations boldly and extract some good from them. But in accepting the God in everything there is a glad meeting and full attentiveness and openness of heart. It is a perfectly happy condition, in which the poet could say:

> Hither! take me, use me, fill me,
> Vein and artery, though ye kill me!

Another way of approaching a knowledge of the heart of the devotee is to ask oneself where the philosopher gets his truth, which is a good. Did he make it? No, he found it. Where did the artist get his beauty? Did he make it? No, he found it. Since it takes the best and greatest men merely to find these goods and present them to others in, at best, an imperfect form, what shall be thought of the original Cause of all the truths and beauties? We naturally bow with great joy before the thought of that Cause.

The *bhakta* or devotee is satisfied with the joy of the consciousness of the presence of Goodness. But he still has also a touch of philosophy—the thought that his own joyous devotion—imperfect as he knows it to be and rejoiceful as he is that he has even a little of it, and perhaps even then only sometimes—will ultimately increase to fill the whole of his life and then be present at all times. Thus devotion is itself another good, and a source of joy.

It is only one step more to the formation of *bhakti-yoga*, a method for increasing the *bhakti*. Religious services are usually a mixture of this with what we shall presently study as the mantra-yoga. They aim at the direction of the feelings, and mix it with ceremonial words and actions. In India there is no collective or congregational worship, but still there are occasional gatherings at which stories are told and songs are sung extolling the exploits of divine Incarnations, or there is singing the names or appellations of Deity. In country places there are often *bhajanas* in which songs are sung containing mostly the names of the deities, to the accompaniment of drums and music, before a statue or a picture representing the divinity. Individual worship appears in daily prayers and in yoga practice.

Why is a separate or outside God adored, reverenced, worshipped? Because he is regarded as the source of wealth and bounty, considered either as an example, or as a giver of material benefits, or at least of divine "grace." It is a question whether the raja-yogi could allow himself this form of devotion, which leans on "goodness." The goal of his being is upright, strong life, happy and free because it is illuminated as to *its own* divine nature and that of *all* the other lives seen around, using other forms. If, then, his goal of life is this happiness, which is the joy of upright, strong life, master of its own small world of body and circumstances, how can he look for help towards that freedom at any stage by what he would call the intoxications or consolations or refuges of religion? Let a man do his small daily task according to his strength of will, love and thought, and all will be well with him. He can be immensely devoted to all the life around him, regarding his neighbor as himself. His refuge from selfishness and the fear it brings exists, but he will not bring into it the unnatural considerations of another and separate life governing or uplifting his own. To him this devotion is a *hatha-yoga*, inasmuch as it depends on another "good," external to himself. Therefore this devotion is often found along with the *hatha* schools of yoga. It comes in also along with concentration in the various *chakras*. The *Gheranda Sanhita* mentions it as one of the means to *samadhi*: "Let him meditate in his own heart upon the proper form of his desired deity; let him meditate with the *bhakti-yoga*, full of the greatest gladness; let him shed tears of happiness." [11]

The flow of unrestrained feeling, even if it means self-abandonment before the recognized glory of the divine, also has its dangers if not balanced by thought and knowledge, as insane asylums testify

---

[11] *Gheranda Sanhitā* vii 14-15.

all over the Western world, and a red record of fanaticism and cruelty witnesses in history; though it is a path that may be followed without special guidance, provided the development of intelligence and will in practical life is not neglected. Many churches and other organizations are busy on this line, but for the most part they miss the point of it because they direct attention to God or his representative as something for the weakling to lean upon or as a fountain of blessing for personal gratification, rather than as something so splendid — a Good beyond all goods — that at the mere sight of it one loses personal desires completely, forgets oneself in the contemplation of it, and adds a new form of ecstasy to the permanent treasures of the soul.

From the Hindu point of view there is an error in the Western idea that grace can come down from above in response to devotion, or, still worse, that higher forces can be brought down by it and by ceremonials. Their view is that by grace we are lifted up, not that anything is brought down. It is akin to the doctrine of intuition. If there is intuition, following upon much thought on a given subject, the field of thought is clarified. Yoga, however, aims at the raising of consciousness above the mind into the clarifier. A crude simile may make this clear; a man owns a car, looks after it and drives it along the road to some destination, and because of that the car is both preserved and used. If the car were left to itself it would rot. Or if it were started up and sent off by itself it would soon meet with an accident. But when it is properly used, the car is still a car; it does not become a man, and the man is still a man and does not become a car. So with the mind. If left to itself it will rot or produce an accident. But what is above mind—the ethical and moral principles—will preserve it and use it well, will harmonize its parts and contents and illumine its path. All are glad of the intuition, but the yogi wants more than that—his consciousness must be raised into the very source of that intuition. One is speaking of the *bhakta*, who is to be himself raised up, not to have his material nature glorified.

The use of *mantras* constitutes another very definite department of occult practices, known in India from the oldest times. *Mantras* are charms, spells, magical formulas, incantations. *Mantra-yoga* is the employment of words so arranged as to produce these effects. It is not usually considered that ordinary people are qualified to make *mantras*, but that the *mantra-yogi* is a person who knows the *mantras* which have been made by great *mantra-karas* (*mantra*-makers) in the past. All the hymns of the Vedas are called *mantras*; those which are metrical and meant to be recited loudly are called "*rich*" (hence *Rig-Veda*), those in prose and to be uttered in a low voice are called "*yajus*" (hence *Yajur-Veda*) and the metrical ones intended for chanting are called *saman* (hence *Sama-Veda*). Mantras are formularies which are meant to produce an effect on people and sometimes on things, which will be so affected that they would then affect people. Thus, for example, *mantras* are useful for consecrating shrines, instruments, vestments and other things. People of Western countries are familiar with the idea, as it occurs not only in their stories or folk-lore about wizards and witches, but also in the practices of some of the churches, in which it is imperative that the priest shall conduct the ceremonies with the words exactly as prescribed, and shall also wear the vestments and make the gestures or movements traditionally associated with them and use the instruments according to rule.

It is to be noted that the prescribed wording and chanting must be accompanied by the right intention and belief in the mind. The *mantra* is not supposed to be effective without the thought which is called the intent or purpose; nevertheless the incantator need not know the meaning of the words employed—it makes no difference to the mantric action whether he knows them or not. But the correct *intention* must be used with the *mantra* belonging to it. This implies that one cannot use a *mantra* for any purpose other than that originally intended. It also indicates that the use of *mantras* is not passive (such as that of prayer-wheels or prayer-flags), but they are considered as tools. Thus the reproduction of a recited *mantra* by gramophone record would have no effect beyond that of its mere sound or music.

There are many different *mantras* associated with different schools of activity. But in all of them the chief feature is the repetition (*japa*) of certain fixed forms of words, often with a definite intonation, and always with the thought of their meaning and intention. We find this practice frequently combined with *bhakti-yoga*, as in the following example, from the *Gopalatapani Upanishad* and the *Krishna Upanishad*. Of all the mantras of Shri Krishna, none is considered more powerful than this five-divisioned, eighteen-syllabled one, which is: "Klim, Krishnaya, Govindaya, Gopi-jana, Vallabhaya, Swaha!" The following is the explanation, translated in my book on Concentration:

> "Once the sages came to the great Brahma and asked: 'Who is the supreme God? Whom does Death fear? Through the knowledge of what does all become known? What makes this world continue on its course?'

> "He replied: 'Shri Krishna verily is the supreme God. Death is afraid of Govinda (Shri Krishna). By knowledge of the Lord of Gopi-jana (Shri Krishna) the whole is known. By Swaha the world goes on evolving.'

"Then they questioned him again: 'Who is Krishna? Who is Govinda? Who is the Lord of Gopi-jana? What is Swaha?'

"He replied: 'Krishna is he who destroys all wrong. Govinda is the knower of all things, who, on earth, is known through the great teaching. The Lord of Gopi-jana is he who guides all conditioned beings. Swaha is his power. He who meditates on these, repeats the *mantra*, and worships him, becomes immortal.'

"Again they asked him: 'What is his form? What is his *mantra*? What is his worship?'

"He replied: 'He who has the form of a protector of cows. The cloud-colored youth. He who sits at the root of the tree. He whose eyes are like the full-blown lotus. He whose raiment is of the splendor of lightning. He who is two-armed. He who is possessed of the sign of wisdom. He who wears a garland of flowers. He who is seated on the center of the golden lotus. Who meditates upon him becomes free. His is the *mantra* of five parts. The first is *Klim Krishnaya*. *Klim* is the seed of attraction. The second is *Govindaya*. The third is *Gopi-jana*. The fourth is *Vallabhaya*. The fifth and last is *Swaha*. *Klim*—to Krishna—to the Giver of Knowledge—to the Lord of the Cowherds—*Swaha*!'

"Om. Adoration to the Universal Form, the Source of all Protection, the Goal of Life, the Ruler of the Universe, and the Universe itself.

"Om. Adoration to the Embodiment of Wisdom, the Supreme Delight, Krishna, the Lord of Cowherds! To the Giver of Knowledge, adoration!"

Such *mantras* as this are full of symbology, which helps the intent. The word *krishna* means the color of the rain cloud, a symbol of protection and beneficence. The cows are the verses of scripture, *Vallabha* means Lord and also Beloved, and the "cow-herd people" are the great sages. The tree is creation or evolution.

Favorite among the *laya-yogis* is the mantra "Om, aim, klim, strim." "Om" is introductory; the other three are called "seed" *mantras*; *aim* being the seed of speech or intelligence, in the first lotus, *klim* the seed *mantra* of love, in the heart lotus, and *strim* the seed *mantra* of power, in the eyebrow lotus. On the *chitrini* canal at these points there are *granthis*, or "knots," which obstruct the advance of *kundalini*. With the aid of these *mantras*, they are broken through. Great results are said to accrue from many repetitions of this *mantra*, which must be said neither too quickly nor too slowly.

The *mantra Om*, which is used at the beginning and end of all prayers, needs special mention. It is considered to have a harmonizing effect, as being the word, or true name, not merely the appellative name, of the "one life without a second." It is composed of three letters, a, u, and m, and can be pronounced with the a and u both distinctly heard, or, as is more usual, with the two blended together as O. The meaning may be derived in the following way. As a is sounded from the throat, it is the beginning of all sounds, and as m is formed by the closing of the lips, it is the end, u being in the middle. Therefore when *Om* is properly sounded with a glide from one letter to the next, it is the complete word. And since sound is creative power, *Om* is not only the natural name of God, but pronunciation of it is a means to harmony with the divine.

The same idea is symbolically represented in the *Shandilya Upanishad*, where the yogi is told to meditate, using the *pranava* that is, *Om*, at the same time thinking of three goddesses: Gayatri, a girl of reddish color, seated on a swan and carrying a mace, who represents the letter a; Savitri, a young woman of white color, mounted on an eagle and carrying a disc, who represents the letter u; and Saraswati, a mature woman of dark color, riding on a bull and carrying a trident, who represents the letter m. Those goddesses are the wives and *shaktis*, or powers, of the three members of the Trinity—Shiva, Vishnu and Brahma—who together constitute the one Brahman. The yogi is told to use the proportions sixteen, sixty-four and thirty-two for breathing during this meditation.

Very closely allied psychologically with the *mantra-yoga* is the practice of art in connection with religious matters. Just as the repetition of certain words helps the devotee to keep his mind well concentrated, so in the case of the temperament which runs to external creativeness, painting and sculpture is a means of holding up and preserving the desired emotional and mental states. The whole process is like damming up a valley and so conserving the water for the constant use of the countryside. Art may be looked upon as a form of yoga. Shukracharya says: "Let the image-maker establish images in temples by meditation on the deities who are the objects of his devotion. In no other way, not even by direct and immediate vision of an actual object, is it possible to be so absorbed in contemplation as thus in the making of images."

Out of this inevitably comes beauty, even when the intention to do so is not intellectually formulated, for action well done always produces that effect in some natural way. Thus, for example, the limbs and figure of the racehorse are wonderfully beautiful because of the skill developed in running, and also the running is beautiful to see. When an artist does his best, the same effect is produced, both in the man and in the work. This itself constitutes a kind of union with the divine, for if it can be said that God is expressible in material form, it must be in beauty, since that is the one thing in the material world of which the soul never tires.

To understand all this theoretically one has to remember that in the use of the senses there are three factors—the conscious being, the sensations (as of color, or sound) and the sense-organ (including the whole mechanism from the eye or the ear to the brain-center). Occultly, the sensations are something in themselves, which the mind carries within itself even away from the body. The objects of the world with their colors etc., are expressions of these sensations in innumerable combinations, brought about through action-organs, and then those objects can arouse the sensations again through the sense-organs.

These sensations are vastly important, because they arouse the attentiveness of the consciousness, and assist its concentration or attentiveness and so enrich its content and power. When consciousness is stronger, clearer, its power is greater. Thus sensations are carriers of the will, both ways—from man to the world and from the world to man. It is easy from this principle to see how all that is going on in this world is a sort of magic. In that magic we get our most formative and delighting effect in what we call beauty, and all things affect us through the shock of beauty or through the lesser process of repetition. Deliberate use of this process is a form of yoga; in the case of the latter method, repetition, we have the mantric effect.

CHPTER 6

THE OCCULT PATH OF BUDDHA

Always the Buddha spoke of two ways of life—one being the ordinary thoughtless

course in which people seek happiness through various pleasures, always hoping that they can obtain conditions which will give them satisfaction, the other being called the Path (as distinguished from the former, which is wandering about), a progressive determination to cease such seeking for pleasure in material things. There is no traveling on this Path, it is stated, for one is not going from one place to another, or even from one mental condition to another. The goal on this path is most occult, hidden from both sense and mind, but is revealed when there is cessation of the ordinary manner of life, which could well be called the way of error and sorrow. The goal is indeed called a ceasing, not a gaining; it is a ceasing of the error or ignorance of desiring and seeking—lo here, lo there. This is called *nibbanna* or *nirvana*.

Before describing the Path we must see what Buddha's great discovery was. It was the discovery that great indescribable joy comes to the man who realizes the universality of sorrow. It comes because he is thereby released from the sense of dependence upon material things and the craving for them. You are clinging to sorrow and suffering. In your ignorance you hug and kiss the spokes of this wheel of agony.

This doctrine was formulated as Four Noble Truths: The Universality of Sorrow or Suffering; The Cause of Sorrow; The Ceasing of Sorrow; and The Way of the Ceasing of Sorrow. We are a little handicapped in using the English language to express the central idea of this doctrine, for we have not one single word, as Buddha had, to express both bodily and psychological suffering, both pain and sorrow. Perhaps suffering will be the best word to use. Perhaps we shall see, if we examine our heart's desire closely, that if we had it fulfilled there would still be suffering. Some may say that they will accept suffering if they can have some pleasure as well. Shelley said that man looks before and after, and longs for what is not, and Shakespeare went further and pointed out that even if man has what he wants, the thought of time with its changes and uncertainties destroys his happiness. And Robert Burns mentioned that in one respect the life of a mouse was happier than that of a man—the present only troubles it. It is here that the revelation of Buddha came in — the assertion that from his own experience there is the incredible joy of nirvana for those who put aside this error of seeking or expecting happiness from circumstances.

Buddha did not leave people to grope their way out of error and craving. His fourth Truth is called a Path — the Noble Eightfold Path. This means that there are eight things to do which, if successfully done, are ways of living without sorrow. We have now to examine this path, remembering always that there can be no cheating, that this path cannot be used for the purpose of attaining something that is within the wheel of sorrow, whether an object of the body or a quality of the mind.

In the naming of the eight requirements of the Path there is a reiteration of the word "correct" or "proper" at the beginning of each. The first four answer the question, "How does the pilgrim comport himself in thought, speech and action on all occasions?" The second four point to special efforts he must make in his life. The first four are as follows:

1. Correct understanding, views, outlook, appraisal, judgment.

2. Correct aims, motives, plans, considerations, decision.

3. Correct use of speech.

4. Correct behavior, conduct or actions.

Analyzing these and other modes of living in my book *Character-Building* many years ago, I reduced all the defects of human nature to three: laziness, selfishness and thoughtlessness, and all virtues to three, action, goodwill and thoughtfulness. These three touchstones are implied in the word "correct" in each of the four requirements. No. I implies that one has at the outset adopted the outlook described by Buddha, what is called the *dhamma* (*dharma*), law, rule, or proper way of life. *Dharma* means maintenance—the maintenance on all occasions, in all matters of life, small or great, of the resolution to put an end to pain, which is the basis of the three virtues of action, goodwill and thoughtfulness. These three are to be followed regardless of pain or trouble. Much stress is laid on speech for it is in this that dissipation of life most commonly occurs—idle chatter, cruel gossip and talk without information.

The second group of four requirements assigns the tasks:

5. Correct mode of livelihood—the fulfilling of a definite role in life, which shall be unselfish, sensible, useful.

6. Correct effort—some work of doing good.

7. Correct intellectual activity—some study.

8. Correct contemplation—the expectant poise of the mind which allows intuition and insight to begin.

All these eight have to do with daily life and the use of personal abilities and energies in the world. They may be pursued with less or greater determination and constancy; as Edwin Arnold puts it in his beautiful poem *The Light of Asia*:

> Strong limbs may dare the rugged road which storms,
> Soaring and perilous, the mountain's breast;
> The weak must wind from slower ledge to ledge,
> With many a place of rest.

> So is the Eightfold Path which brings to peace;
> By lower or by upper heights it goes.
> The firm soul hastes, the feeble tarries. All
> Will reach the sunlit snows.

Now we have to look at the inner or esoteric aspect of all this, and answer the question: "What is happening to the pilgrim himself?" For this purpose Buddha gave the four stages of the Path, and showed what are the defects or "fetters" which bind the ordinary man, and how they are to be thrown off one after the other. The first result of practicing the eightfold way is the weakening and disappearance of the error that the body is itself important. All the eight efforts lead one to be intent upon the life-side of living. It is not a mere intellectual discovery or piece of psychic science which is proposed here. The man will instinctively stop placing bodily interest first in his thoughts. Pleasures and pride in body and personal qualities will be replaced by the eight general life interests. The *second* fetter to go is uncertainty or doubt about this path. The life proves its value as it goes along and great confidence or faith arises from this knowledge and experience. *Third* comes the cessation of dependence upon outward forms or rules or ceremonies. It is the *life* that will speak in this man on all occasions. On life he will depend, and to life he will respond with life. His action will then face the problems which arise, and will be full of both love and thought. Outer rules and forms are for those who are not on this path.

Then fade away the two terrible "fetters" which hold back the ordinary man from almost any semblance of true living: ignorant likes and dislikes—one should say more than this, passionately ignorant likes and dislikes, producing an inflexibility of mind and living which in most cases borders on the psychopathic. Doctors are acquainted with the fact that many people go about in wheel chairs; not because of inability to walk, but inability to think they can; here we have masses of inabilities and dependencies among mankind, including negativeness and fears. But the grip of fixed likings and dislikings loosens its hold on those who are treading the Noble Eightfold Path, and they become ready to meet everything appreciatively according to its nature. All their troubles are then real or material ones; they have ceased making psychological ones in addition—psychological troubles such as discontent, envy, jealousy, resentment, malice, anxiety, worry, impatience, irritability, etc., which do no good, and only hinder the use of the powers of the life in their dealing with the real troubles.

When these five fetters lie in the dust, as the poet puts it, there are still five more. This situation marks the half-way house of the upward Path. The man is now called an Arhat, a word which means "ready" or "qualified." He now knows what he wants and he is competent to go after it. In a secondary meaning he is worthy, admirable, deserving. The five remaining fetters are:

6. Desire for life in form.

7. Desire for formless life.

8. Pride.

9. Self-love.

10. Ignorance.

It would not be fitting here to attempt to say what this final ignorance is, except negatively—it is the conception of oneself as anything conceivable. Perhaps we had better leave it at that, for it is fundamental in Buddha's thought, as in that of Krishna, Shankaracharya, Jesus and all great *gurus* or teachers, that our final union is with something Beyond—beyond the limitations of mind, thought, feelings and the will, all these, as well as bodily things, being limitations. Buddha more than all others impressed this thought constantly upon his hearers, and emphasized the use of the word *nirvana*—which means "to extinguish" as, for example, the blowing out of a candle. But this includes even the extinction of extinction. In Edwin Arnold's words:

> Seeking nothing, he gains all;
> Foregoing self, the Universe grows "I";
> If any teach Nirvana is to cease,
> Say unto such they lie.
>
> If any teach Nirvana is to live,
> Say unto such they err; not knowing this,
> Nor what light shines beyond their broken lamps,
> Nor lifeless, timeless, bliss.

CHAPTER 7

THE CHINESE YOGA

When the Buddha wished to allude to the final achievement or attainment of human life he spoke of *nirvana*, a "blowing-out." This means that in that experience, there will be an absence of our familiar limitations known as body and mind. Even the mind is for us an object of knowledge. The field of our knowledge can be divided into objective and subjective. Both are within the field—both the knower and the known, the subject and the object.

Buddha's doctrine was that only in the presence of knowing are "subject and object" to be seen. Mind with its reasoning activity—its logic—generally considered as the subject, is in reality only an instrument. It does not know. [12] Behind or beyond this mind is what among Chinese Buddhists came to be called Essence of Mind. It is Bodhi, Wisdom. If a

------

[12] In my own terms: there is no such thing as body-consciousness, and no such thing as mind-consciousness, but only, in these cases, consciousness of the body and consciousness of the mind.

man could put aside the error or delusion of the-self-as-mind there would be the elimination of object and subject relation from his experience, and then — *nirvana*.

It was always held that only man can perform this feat, because he—not the lower animals—has mind as *reason*. Of course, there was lower mind, or instinct, in the animals, but this was accumulated knowledge—recognition and memory. And every idea or mental picture in this store of knowledge was accompanied by feeling and therefore by desire. In modern terms we would call this collection the subconscious mind, instinct. The sub-conscious mind could not be regarded as merely a matter of bodily habit. The body is always changing its particles. The incoming particles cannot be regarded as possessing the habits which have been learned by the outgoing particles. So even the continuity of its form is carried on by the "sub-conscious mind"—not by any powers of the body. This continuity governs not only the bodily reactions to environmental impacts, but also the emotions and flow of mental pictures, or association of ideas. So there is instinct. Buddha called this complex of continuity the *skandhas*.

Man has something more than instinct. He has reason, although it must be admitted that very often he acts by instinct, and reason is often if not generally far from its maturity and power.

The height of reasoning or thinking is meditation, called *dhyana* among the old psychologists of India. In a boat, instinct would tell us to row, but reason would tell us to put up a sail, until even the putting up of a sail passed into the sub-conscious and reason led us further to install a motor. Whatever our problem, reason will improve our reaction, but reason demands time—we must think the matter over, consider the nature of water, of boats, of many things involved, study their relations in mental pictures, and then, after this process, which takes time, the problem is solved. Meditation is the complete mental review of the materials of the problem and the study of their combination. It is applied to ordinary material problems and to the most abstruse psychological and philosophical ones.

But this does not tell the whole story of meditation. If properly carried out it ends up with intuition— something you did not know before, and have not found in the world. This is sometimes called *prajna*. This intuition is not reason, but is direct perception, and the state of the mind in which this *prajna* or intuition is in power is called *samadhi*, which literally taken means completely in agreement or order. This experience by direct perception is called in China and Japan a *satori*. But I am running ahead. Let us first look at the way in which the mind gets knowledge for us.

Mind is called "sixth sense." By mind we get to know things not available to the senses of hearing, touching, seeing, tasting and smelling. It can operate in three stages, and usually does—through testimony, reasoning and seeing for ourselves. Someone comes into the house and says there is a fire on the mountain; this is supported by reason, because there is smoke; then we can go and find the fire—and perhaps put it out. So there is testimony and then reasoning and then direct perception. This applies in religious matters. Buddha says he has found joy and knowledge; it is reasonable; we are to go and find it.

When the *dhyana* or meditation process was carried into China by the famous Indian "missionary" Bodhidharma, it came to be known as *Chan*, and a little later when it had found its way to Japan the word was further modified and became *Zen*. *Zen* is Japanese meditation-yoga.

It is not to be thought that in either India or China the results of *dhyana* were merely improved subjective experience. In India the fruit of *samadhi* was *viveka* or discrimination, which means a *new valuation*. This is stated emphatically by Patanjali in his aphorism no. ii 28, which describes the final effect of the performance of the eight Limbs of Yoga, culminating in *samadhi*. This is not a perfection of the subjective, but a transcendence of the subjective conception of the subject-object relation. Subject and object now live together in the Knowing or Consciousness in a new way. Subject-self is overcome. It was a piece of Ignorance, a five-branched tree of ignorance.

In the case of Buddha we have exactly the same teaching, when *avidya*, ignorance, is given as the final "fetter" to be cast off, as shown in our previous chapter. This was essentially ignorance or error about self or the subjective entity.

It is natural that the method of practice of the *Chan* and the *Zen* should be somewhat different from that in India, as befits the racial types of China and Japan. The method is well described in *The Sutra of Wei Lang*, translated by Wong Mou-Lam, [13] and in Christmas Humphreys' *Zen Buddhism*, [14] and in several books by Professor D. T. Suzuki.

Before we turn to the practices of *Zen* it is necessary

---

[13] Published for the Buddhist Society, London, by Luzac & Co., Ltd.

[14] Published for the Buddhist Society, London, by Luzac & Co., Ltd.

to say that the fundamental conceptions associated with it are also found in the old Tao-ism of China, coming down even from Lao Tsu, who lived about the same time as Buddha. Buddhism became blended with this. The difference was that Buddha desired not to give a name to *nirvana*, as that would almost inevitably lead to some mental idea of it, which would then stand in the way of the transcendental experience. Even the idea of transcendence does so.

In the old teaching there was *Tao*, the motionless, master of all, both the subjective and objective sides of Nature, including man. It could equally be called the absolute motion, which, passing through every point of space in every direction in every moment of time, becomes the ever-present soul of all motions, but is motionless from the standpoint of the subject-object world.

From *Tao* come *yang* and *yin*, the active and passive sides of Nature, light and shadow. In man the two elements appear as intellect and instinct. The instinct-flow is natural, outward-going, but the intellect-flow, which is "backward-going, reversed, turned round," can become so pure that it gains release, when things are recognized but not desired. *The Secret of the Golden Flower*, translated by Richard Wilhelm, gives the lay-out of principles, and is a splendid source-book for this study.

Introspectively, all can see that knowledge and desire go opposite ways. Desire draws man into complicated experiences, bringing problems which can be solved only by the intellect seeing things as they are, untainted by desires concerning them. The path of yoga, in this field, thus means knowing or seeing without desire. There is, of course, knowing, or consciousness, in both cases. The animal is highly conscious, but instinctual; in man the consciousness is becoming intellectual; in the *bodhisattwa* (which means one whose intellect is pure, or whose very nature is intellect) we have man on the verge of *nirvana*, or *Tao*. In all three cases feeling and knowledge go hand in hand. Where there is pure knowledge, the feeling is love—love without desire, full consciousness and approach completely without antagonism. This is the *Zen* outlook, whatever terminology of China or India, of *Tao* or Buddhism may be used. The practice of meditation in this field is "seeing without desire." And the height of it is reached when there is direct perception, intuition in which reasoning stops. There is no *desire* for logic to stop; it does so naturally when its function is fulfilled; then intuition appears.

If we compare the art of China with that of Greece we find that one is more the product of imaginative observation, the other of introspectional observation. The word imaginative here means image-making. It is less creative and more contemplative. If the poise of the Chinese has the relative proportions shown in diagram A, that of the Indo-European is relatively somewhat as in diagram B.

The difference of different minds, and races of men, is a difference in the proportions and status of these three. I have cited art here because art is yoga in action, action free from the taint of desire and utility or use. It gives us a peep-hole into the mind. So the meditation-systems of China did not develop on very introspectional lines, as meditation in Europe has done.

In *The Secret of the Golden Flower* a form of meditation is given in which a super-physical self is built. Intellect or the light of seeing is to be freed from the instinctual, is to build a body of its own. This is done by stopping the flight of thoughts—concentrate, but quickly pass into contemplation; when contemplation falls into flights again, renew the concentration. This "circulates" the process—brings it into circle, not *drives* it round, but puts an end to wandering off. As in India, attention is to be given at first to the body—body comfortable, breathing rhythmic, senses quiet. Then one listens within, to the no-sound, listens to the silence. Thus within the heart another "body" is gradually built up, which is a spiritual body.

Though many details are given in *The Secret of the Golden Flower* there is no room for them here;

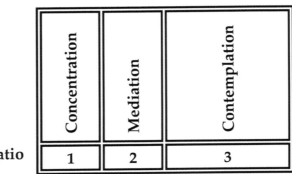

Diagram A (CHINA)

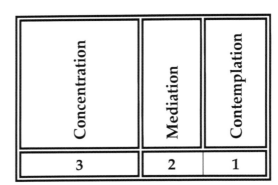

Diagram B (EUROPE)

It is to be understood, of course, that while this rotary motion is the same for all sane minds, the standard or evolutionary status is individual. In the individual there is growth through use of exercise, whereby each of the three elements is advanced in ability. Taking this into consideration, it will be seen that the movement is spiral as well as rotary.

besides, the serious student will supply his own details. It is the body or focus of knowing (Confucius), of the heart-view (Buddha), of inward vision (Lao Tsu). The intuition will come; one must hardly ask for it, and certainly not presuppose its nature. The magical material side of it will be that the new "body" will be the intuition-vehicle for living free from the space-limitation of the body, and so, being concerned with seeing and doing remote from the body, giving what may be called a practical or objective side also to the intuition, which is not one-sided but concerns object as well as subject.

Buddha said: "Nor sink the string of thought into the Fathomless." But men cannot leave it at that; they strive to realize the truth. Buddha does not object to that, but says it will not be done by thought. Intuition which is not thought will do it. But intuition comes to us; we do not make it. Is it different from the objective, or different from the subjective? We must answer, "No," because difference is a thought, a comparison, an attribute. So not by the suppression of the world or the mind is intuition to be sought. Without their absence comes this something which they as such cannot present. They would not be themselves without it. Ordinarily the mind is taken up with objective or subjective interests and activities, leaving no opening for the third. When people seek that third, intellectual desire is usually present, even if instinctual desire has been overcome. The first point of *Zen* meditation is therefore, "Drop it!" Any means which will start the process and thwart the intellectual desire will be permissible, provided it does not prevent the "Go on" or, if there is a teacher, the "Come on!" which is like that of a mother calling a young child to walk, without a word about the mechanism of walking.

Three techniques have been specially prominent in the schools of *Zen*—the wall-gazing, the sudden question (*mondo*) and the enigmatic statement (*koan*). The first is not gazing at a wall, as one might think, but gazing like a wall. You are the wall, upright to the world, set by the plumb-line of your own nose, unaffected, intent on the Essence of Mind. Bodhidharma is said to have practiced this for nine years, avoiding commitments and desires, like an upright wall. He taught for fifty years in China. The sixth Patriarch in his succession was Hui-neng, or Wei-Lang, through whom Chinese Buddhism, harmonized with the *Tao*, emerged as a definite way of life, allowing no dogmas, requiring an enquiring mind, searching within, demanding humble faith in the coming of sudden enlightenment, and— materially—a simple life of self-restraint, industry and sympathy.

Teachings of Buddha much used by the founders of the *Zen* sect were: the *Lankavatara Sutra*, the

Avatansaka Sutra, the *Surangama Sutra,* the *Mahayana Shraddhotpada Shastra* and the *Diamond Sutra.* To these were added the *Sutra* of Wei-Lang. The whole collection is very conveniently gathered together and presented in Goddard's *Buddhist Bible.* [15]

The teaching of meditation in the *Diamond Sutra* prescribes sitting alone, erect, motionless, quieting the mind, with attention on no definite thing, excluding recollection and imagination, abandoning all notions of an external world, turning to inner intuitive consciousness, gradually entering *samadhi,* ideal tranquility, and thus passing from vagrant thinking and even intellectual activity into the realization of insight.

It was especially among the Chinese and Japanese that the sudden enlightenment was brought about by sudden means. Intuition is by its very nature always sudden—not built up—but sudden means or methods were also now brought in, in the shape of *koans* and *mondos.*

The *koan* is a mind-baffling statement to be meditated upon. The teacher requires an answer; there is no hurry about it, but you are expected to

---

[15] Published by E. P. Dutton and Co., New York.

tackle it, and to stick at it until you have a solution. The statement is of such a nature that the intellect cannot understand it, and all its efforts to do so are in vain. It is thus thwarted and nullified, and the yogi must therefore sweat and strain, so to speak, with great will power until an intuitive answer comes. It is very strenuous, and dangerous unless the *koan* is given by a competent teacher to an appropriate student. The intuition is such that it cannot be expressed in words, but when it comes there will be a lighting-up of the mind which will cause an involuntary exclamation or action, such as the laugh or the slap of the thigh which one gives when there is a sudden seeing of the point of a joke or the solution of a conundrum, and one says, "I never thought of *that*."

As an example, the teacher may say: "You have knees, you have feet. Come, let us fly." Or, a classical one, "The two hands clap with a noise; listen to the clap of one hand." There should be no agreed upon, traditional or conventional meaning to these *koans*. They may be invented *ad lib*. A good example occurs accidentally, as it were, in the *Glorious Presence* where, after expounding the Vedantic doctrine of "Not thus, not thus" from the commentary on the *Mundukya Upanishad* where Gaudapada says: "There is no limitation, no creation, no bondage, no maker, no aspirant, nobody freed—this is the correct knowledge," the continuation is: "And no 'no,' and there we are." Another example occurred when the Sixth Patriarch wrote his first statement: in reply to:

> Our body is the Bodhi-tree,
> And our mind a mirror bright.
> Carefully we wipe them hour by hour,
> And let no dust alight.

His stanza said:

> There is no Bodhi-tree,
> Nor stand of a mirror bright.
> Since all is void,
> Where can the dust alight?

The last two lines form a perfect *koan*.

The resulting enlightenment is called a *satori*. This "goal" as well as the method is called *Zen*, just as in India yoga means both the practice and the attainment. Mr. Christmas Humphreys thus explains it: "Zen is not an escape from things but a new way of looking at things, whereby they are seen to be already in Nirvana." [16] We are denying ourselves, which is the great Error. Still, one must take care not to call *Zen* or *Nirvana* a state; for that conception, or any conception, is within the *maya* or error. Nor "looking."

The *mondo* is question and answer. Here there is no continued wrestling as it were in terrible unmental

---
[16] *Zen Buddhism*, by Christmas Humphreys, p. 95

attentiveness, as in the case of the *koan*. An immediate answer is required, without thought. It will be noticed that this is another way of side-stepping the thought process while maintaining the attentiveness. For example, a *Zen* master once held out a stick and said, "Call it not a stick; if you do you assert. Nor deny that it is a stick; if you do, you negate. Without affirmation or denial, speak, speak!" It is not recorded what the pupils said, but I tried this on myself and out came "On, on!" And this carried knowledge, like a dream.

Life sets us *koans* and *mondos* all the time, for never do we know enough to act with full intelligence. As far as we ourselves are concerned:

> All things are rushing to their doom;
> Trying to slow the rush
> The mind preserves their death.

CHAPTER 8

THE SUFI YOGAS

As is fitting in the field of a religion based upon the revelations through the Prophet Muhammad, the practices (or yogas) and fulfilments of the Sufis were and are entirely saturated with the doctrine of Islam, which is resignation to God, or rather delighted union of the will of man with the will of God. This fundamental principle of acceptance of God's *will* among the religious becomes the reception of God's *being* among the mystics.

In the efforts and attainments of these mystics must be recognized therefore *two* operators—God who is trying to give himself to man, and man who is trying to give himself to God. The second of these factors, the human efforts, naturally takes on the aspect of yoga practice—purification of the self from worldly desires, mental defects and selfish motives, often by means of frequent deep and prolonged meditation, and even by physical asceticism, intended in some cases to reduce the body to submission, and in others to demonstrate submission achieved.

It was indeed from one of these practices that the very name "Sufi" was adopted—the wearing of woolen garments by these mystics and yogis, a mild equivalent of the Christian hair shirt. The word "sufi" is derived from a word meaning wool.

The foundations of the contrast between material riches and the presence of God which has had great influence in the Sufi life were laid by Muhammad himself, when he said "Poverty is my pride," and rejected the personal use of riches, as well as in the example of earlier Prophets, including Moses, David and Jesus. Many were the Sufi ascetics and mystics who gave up wealth and pursued the simple life.

It was, however, always the constant thought or remembrance (*dhikr*) of God that was considered the means to Union (*tauhid*) with Him, in which there was the passing away (*fana*) of all the human qualities or human nature, the only continuity (*bava*) being then the continuity of God Himself. Students of comparative yoga will see in this a similarity to Buddha's doctrine of *Nibbanna*, or *Nirvana*, in the achievement of which every vestige of what man can think or feel himself to be entirely disappears. This transformation of the Sufi could take place during life, but woe to the man who might say that he had become God. The true idea is quite different from that. It is a dying to self. The orthodox of Islam would never allow a man to call himself God, or permit the idea that God would appear in or through human form. All its inspirers were regarded only as Prophets, of whom Muhammad was the greatest, and the height of their message was loss of self in God. When man is lost in God, the continuity is God's, not man's.

The technicalities of Sufi yoga practice were never codified with the exactitude found among the Hindus and Buddhists, though it must be said that Sufi teachers in India sometimes adopted portions of the Hindu meditational methods, without abating the essential aim of devotional submission. The present writer became acquainted with one Sufi teacher in the north of India who had sixteen thousand disciples or followers within a radius of about fifty miles, and was using methods of meditation the same as those of one of the Hindu schools. This brings to attention the fact that although there are many "sannyasi" Sufis wandering about with musical instruments and singing devotional songs, still the bulk were and are people in ordinary occupations, as is the case with Hindu aspirants also.

Music plays an important part in the life of most of the Sufis in India, following the Mevlavi Order established by Maulana Jatal al-Din Rumi. It is not only through the eye that things can tell us of their essential being. To go along with the experiences in perfect harmony, even unity, is the height of a sort of meditation which conveys experience beyond thought and reason. Every being acts from its own character, and usually the seeing or experiencing is limited to the material gain—so a worm sees a tree in one way, a bird in another, a monkey in another, a worldly man in another. But a spiritual man must see it in another way, without the antagonism and conquesting of his reasoning mind, but with acceptance, harmony and flowing—with, in short, a sort of meditativeness which excludes reason. On this account the allegories of Love and Wine came to fill the poetry of the Sufis. Thus one can understand stanza 60 of Omar Khayyam's *Rubaiyat*:

> You know, my friends, with what a brave carouse
> I made a second marriage in my house,
> Divorced old barren Reason from my bed
> And took the Daughter of the Vine to spouse.

In this sort of meditativeness or lovefull attentiveness there is experience above reason, above expression in words. This was usual with Emerson, so he could write:

> Cans't thou copy in verse one chime
> Of the wood-bell's peal and cry,
> Write in a book the morning's prime,
> Or match with words that tender sky?
>
> Wonderful verse of the gods,
> Of one import, of varied tone;

130

They chant the bliss of their abodes
To man imprisoned in his own.

Ever the words of the gods resound;
But the porches of man's ear
Seldom in this low life's round
Are unsealed, that he may hear.

Moulana Rumi expressed the longing of Love in the
following verses translated by R. A. Nicholson in his
book *Rumi, Poet and Mystic*:

Hearken to this Reed forlorn,
Breathing, ever since 'twas born
From its rushy bed, a strain
Of impassioned love and pain.

The secret of my song, though near,
None can see and none can hear.
Oh, for a friend to know the sign
And mingle all his soul with mine!

'Tis the flame of Love that fired me,
'Tis the wine of Love inspired me.
Woulds't thou learn how lovers bleed,
Hearken, hearken to the Reed!

It is part of the technique of Sufism to be on guard
not to fail in this Love, or unantagonistic looking, in
oneself as in all. There is no self-fighting in this.
Look with Love, and the divine "intoxication" of the
Wine will come. As Rumi, again, said:

131

Into my heart's night
Along a narrow way
I groped; and lo! the light,
An infinite land of day.

This awareness of the real man is put in less direct terms in the poem on *Body and Soul* by another Persian poet, Enweri—translated in Emerson's essay on Persian Poetry:

A painter in China once painted a hall;
Such a web never hung on an emperor's wall;—
One half from his brush with rich colors did run,
The other he touched with a beam of the sun;
So that all which delighted the eye in one side,
The same, point for point, in the other replied.
In thee, friend, that Tyrian chamber is found;
Thine the star-pointing roof, and the base on the ground:
Is one half depicted with colors less bright?
Beware that the counterpart blazes with light!

"Beware" means, of course, "be aware."

We may find room in this short introduction to Sufi yoga for two verses, vi 17-18—very percipient—from Richard Burton's *Kasidah*:

Yes Truth may be, but 'tis not Here; mankind must seek and find it There,
But Where nor *I* nor *you* can tell, nor aught earth-mother ever bare.

Enough to think that Truth can be: come sit we where
the roses glow,
Indeed he knows not how to know who knows not
also how to unknow.

Cease, then, your own Almighty Power to bind, to
bound, to understand.

In his book *Sufism*, Prof. A. J. Arberry gives a list of
the meanings of terms used in much of the Sufi love-
poetry, compiled from a treatise by Muhsin Faid
Kashani, a Persian author of two centuries ago.
Among these are the Face or Cheek (Divine Beauty,
Grace, Bounty, Light, Reality), the Tresses (Majesty,
Power, the veil of Reality), Mole (point of Unity),
Eye and Glance (God's beholding and granting),
Eyebrow (the attributes which veil the Essence),
Wine (ecstatic experience), Wine-bearer (Reality,
loving to manifest itself in every form), Cup, Pitcher
and Jar (revelations of Divine Acts, Names and
Qualities), Sea and Ocean (revelations of Divine
Essence), Tavern (Pure Unity)—but see Professor
Arberry's book for a fuller list and details.

In the Sufi yoga it is separation (*tauhid*) that is to be
overcome. Every aspirant is free to follow the means
of his own choice to this end, with or without the
technique of any particular teacher. Professor
Arberry has given lists of the "stations" reached by
the aspirant's own endeavours and the "states"
which he receives from God, these not being in the
power of human nature to produce for itself,

133

according to three of the ancient writers. The simplest of these lists is that of al-Sarraj, who gives seven "stations"—the conversion from formal religion to the resolution to achieve, abstinence from unnecessary and unsuitable activities, renunciation of pleasures, poverty, patience, trust in God and satisfaction—and ten "states"—meditation, nearness to God, love, fear, hope, longing, intimacy, tranquillity, contemplation and certainty. 1

The part played by music in the devotional yoga of the Sufis has been told very beautifully by Inayat Khan in his *Mysticism of Sound*. Moulana Rumi especially valued the help of music, so it came strongly into the devotions of the Mevlavi Order of Sufis. A branch of this order came to India, and was carried to great heights by Khaja Moinudin Chisti. For many centuries at his tomb in Ajmere there has always been and still is the best of music and singing to be heard. At some of the assemblies of this order, the ecstasy (*Wajad*) of union has three degrees of attainment—objective, ideal and ecstatic. When this ecstasy comes, sometimes it manifests itself in tears, sometimes in sighs, sometimes in actions.

Although this takes place practically there is also a theory of the abstract or unlimited sound, for which the devotee can listen anywhere in nature. This also involves the method of abstractedness through sound which we find among the Hindus as well as the Sufis. This sound has ten forms, it is said, in ten different channels of the human body; it may be like thunder, the roar of the sea, bells, running water, bees, sparrows, the lute, a whistle, a conch-shell, and, highest of all, the sound of *Hu*. The last is found dwelling in all the other sounds as their spirit, as it were. Like the Om of the Hindus, it is regarded as the name of the Nameless, constantly sounded by Nature. When ecstasy comes the Sufi forgets mental as well as physical existence. The effect, however, is throughout; body and mind are purified and made able to receive intuitions.

In writing even briefly of the aims and techniques of the Sufis one must not omit the dancing or whirling of the Dervishes, not seen in India, but in Egypt and some other countries. These take various forms, as shown by E. W. Lane in his *Manners and Customs of the Modern Egyptians*. Remembrance (*zikr*) accompanies the practice, in the form of repetitions of the "Allah," with or without additional exclamations. The following is an extract from Lane:

> The durweeshes, who formed the large ring (which enclosed four of the marble columns of the portico) now commenced their zikr; exclaiming over and over again, "Allah!" and, at each exclamation, bowing the head and body, and taking a step to the right; so that the whole ring moved rapidly round. As soon as they commenced this exercise, another durweesh, a Turk, of the order of Mowlawees, in the middle of the circle, began to whirl; using both his feet to effect this

135

motion, and extending his arms; the motion increasing in velocity until his dress spread out like an umbrella. He continued whirling thus for about ten minutes; after which he bowed to his superior, who stood within the great ring; and then, without showing any signs of fatigue or giddiness, joined the durweeshes in the great ring; who had now begun to ejaculate the name of God with greater vehemence, and to jump to the right, instead of stepping. After whirling, six other durweeshes, within the great ring, formed another ring; but a very small one; each placing his arms upon the shoulders of those next him; and thus disposed, they performed a revolution similar to that of the larger ring, except in being much more rapid; repeating, also, the same exclamation of "Allah!" but with a rapidity proportionately greater. This motion they maintained for about the same length of time that the whirling of the single durweesh before had occupied; after which, the whole party sat down to rest. They rose again after the lapse of about a quarter of an hour; and performed the same exercises a second time.

Prefacing his poem *Song of Seid Nimetollah of Kuhistan*, Emerson has a note on another form of this dance, as follows:

Among the religious customs of the dervishes is an astronomical dance, in which the dervish imitates the movements of the heavenly bodies, by spinning on his own axis, whilst at the same time he revolves round the Sheikh in the centre, representing the sun; and, as he spins, he sings the Song of Seid Nimetollah of Kuhistan.

The first portion of the Song tells what state of mind the dancers are trying to reach:

> Spin the ball! I reel, I burn,
> Nor head from foot can I discern,
> Nor my heart from love of mine,
> Nor the wine-cup from the wine.
> All my doing, all my leaving,
> Reaches not to my perceiving;
> Lost in whirling spheres I rove,
> And know only that I love.

*   *   *

Other similar books in the subject area published by Indo-European Publishing include:

RAJA YOGA OR MENTAL DEVELOPMENT: A SERIES OF LESSONS IN RAJA YOGA

By YOGI RAMACHARAKA

&

How To Be A Yogi, Including a Chapter Titled: "Was Christ a Yogi?"

By Swami Abhedananda